THESEUS BOOKS

www.theseusbooks.com

A Theseus Books paperback.

Published in the UK by Theseus Books.
This edition published in 2014.

ISBN: 978-1492762874

Dirty Old Man (A True Story)

Moll French

THESEUS BOOKS

I dedicate this book to all survivors of abuse and to all the people who have been affected, either directly or indirectly by it, no matter how far along they are in their recovery.

"Don't let your silence drown out their cries."

Table of Contents

Chapter One.

My family huddled close by with bated breath. It was a conversation they'd have to hear to believe because at that moment, I was an attention seeking liar as far as they were concerned. Sickness flooded the pit of my stomach, and a cold sweat which escaped every pore took its grip upon me.
I sat with my back to the family, though I envisioned their common faces and their expressions of disgust only too well. There would be, 'I can't believe she's fabricated such a story,' and, 'she's so deluded, she must be mentally ill.'
Bernie, was such a well-respected, well-liked family friend, my recent admission had shaken the family to its core.

On the last ring, Bernie answered in his nasally voice, speaking over the crackling connection.
"Hello?"
I hesitated for a moment, until my dad prompted a reply with a rough shove on the back of my head. I cleared my dry throat.
"Hello, it's me." My voice crackled with a dry hoarseness.
"Are you okay Petal?"
The line was silent.
"No, not really."
"Why, what's up?"
My dad gave another rough shove and I flinched.

1

"They know everything." I said, as I tried to compose my shaking voice. "Every single little thing."

"Oh," was all he offered as a reply.

I immediately detected his self-preservative tone and I felt isolated, as though it was my fault I'd landed him in it.

Anxiety darted to every safe corner of my imagination and I worried that when the conversation was over, when I'd put the receiver down; it would be me, versus my family.

Bernie could deny everything of course and dismiss the every word, even put it down to me being a disturbed child, and perhaps it would be plausible enough for my family to believe.They certainly didn't believe my current version of events.

I didn't want to hang up the phone and sever my contact with the world outside, so long as I just stayed on the line I felt no harm would come to me. I'd really left myself open to punishment this time. I wept quietly as the receiver slipped in my perspiring hands.

"Are you on your own? What have your parents said? Are they angry with us?"

It seemed he was testing the water to see if he could deny it, unaware of the loudspeaker. His voice was dry, distinguished by his overly pronounced words that clicked as he spoke. Bernie was the only person I felt able to rely on and my pillar of strength sounded more like a scared rodent at the end of the line.

I finally understood what it meant to open a can of worms.

My dad snatched the receiver away and turned off the hands free, much to the disappointment of the spectators that had gathered.

"Angry? I've not even started to get angry yet!" he spat. "You're a dirty old man, and if you even think of coming near my house again, I'll go up into my attic and bring my gun down. I don't care how long you've been teaching martial arts or how tough you claim to be, nobody can stop a bullet."

Dad silenced for what seemed an eternity and I tried to make out what was being said. It was distorted, wild, and out of my control now. My racing heart threatened to jump up into my throat and choke me at any moment and I'd have welcomed it. My skin was clammy and both palms were sweating. I didn't dry them on my sleeves, I didn't dare move a muscle. I felt it was part of my impending punishment to sit in discomfort because I deserved it.

"Of course I'm threatening you. I thought you were supposed to be intelligent?" Dad scoffed. "She's only fifteen, you're thirty nine. You're twenty four years older than her. There's a name for your sort." He paused momentarily.

"Hang on, hang on just a moment," he said, as he looked towards my mum. "Just how long has this been going on for?" He paused again, his eyes widening with rage.

"Come on, how long?" he shouted.

His answer from the line, (if any), had proven to be unsatisfactory so he turned his attention to me.

"You!" He thrust his finger in my face. "You disgusting tart, how long?"

I didn't say a word - I couldn't. The words were shrivelled stuck in my throat and the adrenaline rode my breath in waves. I felt likely to vomit.

"How long?" he shouted, as he took a swipe at my face.

"Three years." I told him as best I could with a dry croak. "It started around three years ago."

The glares came from every corner of the room and pressed upon me like a dead weight.

My mum sat perched on the edge of her chair with her all too familiar expression of revolt for me. I could see her shutting down, which meant there'd be no support from her. Just when I thought things couldn't get any worse, my dad switched to his game playing strategy. Something that I was also familiar with.

He was now in a position to intimidate someone he once respected and looked up to, and he liked that. This was more like the dad I knew. Not the supportive, caring, protective father I needed at that moment, but rather a game playing, manipulative monster.

"I suggest you get round here and explain yourself," he said. "If you don't come over right now, I'm calling the police."

He slammed the phone down and grinned wickedly at me.

I began to hyperventilate through the tears of humiliation as they streamed down my burning cheeks.

"You can cut that out right now, Madam," said Mum. She told my siblings to make themselves scarce in their rooms, and not to come down unless told otherwise.

Dad had always been fascinated by the military, though unfortunately he lacked the backbone to join. He ran our lives and our home like a boot-camp. There were curfews for every event, and consequences for everybody if something happened and the guilty party didn't own up. He craved feeling in complete control, likely because his own life was so out of control. Having a large family gave him the resources.

There were army cargo nets hung about the house, and a huge mural of a woodland pasted onto one of the walls in the living room. That mural is still vivid in my mind. Mostly because I'd frequently peel sections off, and my dad would make us bring all the varying shades of green crayons we possessed to touch it back up again. The attic was filled with all manner of weapons: shotguns, rifles, hunting knives and crossbows, all things he'd collected at the expense of the tax payer, as he decided he was no longer fit to work because of a bad back and nervous disposition. He'd spent some of his younger years locked up in a mental institute because he'd experimented with far too many drugs during the sixties and seventies.

"But Mum!" protested my sister, Beth, as she walked towards the door.

"It's not a bloody freak show, now get up to your rooms," she said, in a tone dry of any emotion. "And you madam," she pointed at me. "You sit there and don't move even a bit, you'll do exactly as your dad tells you. What he says goes."

She always took his side when it came to me. I don't think she was afraid of him, but her life had become a vicious circle of working to support the family, coming home every night to a messy house, and Dad not progressing any further with his own life. He simply existed in the house, smoking my mum's wages away each day.

We all secretly wanted her to leave him, we fantasised about spending more time with her when it happened, but it was difficult in those days. It was hard enough to survive as it was, and things had become reasonably stable as far as money was concerned. Mum worked two jobs as a cleaner, and Dad received his benefits every week. Money he'd save up for military related items such as binoculars and image intensifiers, enabling him to see in the dark during his nightly woodland escapades.

Alex, my brother, and Beth slipped past me triumphantly. I was going to be in deep trouble. Alex made eye contact as he took his turn out the door.

"Slag," he hissed, and spat in my face. It would be the only occasion where could use such profanity within earshot of our parents without consequences, so he seized the opportunity with no repercussions. Our parents had far more important things on their mind.

Dad left and I sat in silence, listening to him moving about in the next room. My mum barely looked at me, but spoke quietly in a threatening tone.

"You're disgusting, even your brothers and sisters think so. You're a disgrace to this family anyway but you've gone too far this time, Madam. You're tearing up this family."
My heart wanted to leap out of my chest and slither over to my mum, and show her how broken and shrunken it was becoming, eventually it would slither away and die in a dark corner of the room along with dignity and respect.

I jumped as Dad backed loudly into the living room carrying a chair. It was one of his game props; his favourite game was interrogation. He moved the coffee table aside and placed the chair in the middle of the room where Bernie would be sitting. He angled it towards the window because it was a sunny day, and he lowered the seating position. Bernie would have to squint to make out Dad's silhouette against the window. It was a technique he'd picked up from one of his 'The Art of Intimidation' type books that he frequently read during the daytime hours, whilst the world was outside working hard to support people like him.

We waited in silence for Bernie's blue Sierra estate to pull up onto the driveway.

"At least you weren't lying, I'll give you credit for that at least," he said, growing increasingly excited as he anticipated Bernies arrival. Mum said nothing, the silent treatment was bad enough, but it would get worse when she eventually broke her silence,Mum always spoke her truth whether it was right or wrong.

Bernie's car pulled onto the driveway and Dad met him at the door. They spoke not a single word as he led Bernie to his seat. The scene would have been laughable had it not been for the seriousness of it all.

"I'll start shall I?" said Dad. "We found *this* stuffed under Moll's bed this morning, Beth found it."

He pulled out a crumpled letter that had been written on blue paper. I recognised it straight away. I felt both angry and ashamed that my snot faced little sister and my parents had been reading the things I'd written about them. Dad read not the entire letter, but selected parts he was particularly appalled by.

"Living here is like hell on Earth; my family hates me and take everything out on me. I can't wait until I'm old enough to leave home." He mimicked my voice in a stupid fashion and continued. *"It can only be compared to being surrounded by patients in a mental hospital. There's a severe lack of*

8

intelligence and complete ignorance to right and wrong." He looked over at me with his eyebrows raised. *"Thank you for the flowers, I hid them in my school bag like you said, I had to pretend they were from somebody at school, and they teased me about it for ages. I know you said you'd send me something in the post, but I'd rather you didn't because they go through my mail."*

My parents glared at me from their lowered brows as though it was untrue. Dad screwed up the piece of paper and threw it at Bernie, who let it sit on the floor as a constant reminder of my shame and invasion of privacy.

"If Beth hadn't found that letter, you two would never have been caught out, so you have her to thank for that. What do you have to say for yourselves?"
Bernie shrugged, and Dad enjoyed watching as he squirmed in the chair.

Bernie was wearing a padded tartan jacket as he always did, (even my dad started to dress like him after a short while because he idolised him). His too short trousers were held up by a pair of braces, and you could clearly see his white sport socks. It looked as though his shoes had had an arguments with his trousers. His beard was black and bushy, and his long straggly hair was scooped back into a messy, greying ponytail, that reached the middle of his back. His eyes were the colour of the sky before a storm.

9

He fiddled impatiently in his chair, looking about the unusual living room, gazing the strange mural of the woodland on the wall, where a noticeable green felt tip pen had been used to touch up one of the scuffs.

"Look Jim, I don't know what you expect me to say, if you're going to call the police then do it sooner rather than later." His gaunt face was as white as a sheet, and I felt invisible because he hadn't once looked in my direction.

"I'll do it in my own time, not because you say so. You can't manipulate me, Bernie," he said.

I found myself feeling naive and lost in adult conversation, I didn't understand why the police had been mentioned, I didn't think a crime had been committed. I'd been groomed to believe it was all perfectly normal. If it were a crime, then I was directly involved and in big trouble. I chewed my nails nervously and wondered if I'd be sent to prison. I was nearing my GCSE's and couldn't afford to be locked away.

"You've been having a disgusting, not to mention *illegal*, relationship together and it sickens me to my stomach. She was twelve years old when you set your sights on her. I want to know what was going through your mind, and why you can't find a woman your own age."
Dad mocked as he spoke and appeared more interested in humiliating Bernie, seemingly pleased with his new air of authority.

"My personal life is none of your damn business Jim," said Bernie, as he rolled his eyes. "I've done nothing wrong. I've helped her and been there when she needed somebody to talk to, if anything you should be thanking me."

"So you're playing the responsible adult now then are you?"

"She needs someone responsible around her don't you think? You've hardly been a role model have you? I've heard stories about you Jim, you can hardly go around calling me a pervert can you?"

The conversation had been brought to stalemate with Dad momentarily crestfallen, so he tried in vain to change the subject. Bernie beat him to it, taking the power away.

"She will be sixteen in two weeks, she'll be legally old enough to do as she pleases then."

"And just what do you think she'll want to do?" Dad raised his voice again and I sat quietly watching as they verbally sparred back and forth.

"Well it's evident she can't carry on living here. She'll have to move out. I'm moving back to Peterborough in a couple of weeks, if she wants to move in with me then that's up to her."

I felt as though I'd been slapped around the face, Bernie had mentioned moving away, but I didn't think he was serious. I felt deceived and lost. Not for a moment did I suspect that it may have been a premeditated move to get me to run away with him. I was young and naive, and knew nothing much of life beyond school or my own front garden really.

11

"Is this what you want then, Moll?" mocked
Dad. You want tto live with your paedo martial arts
teacher in Peterborough?"
With my head in my hands, I prayed it would all
just stop, I didn't know what a paedo was really.
Well I kind of knew it had something to do with
kids but as a child myself, I understood nothing of
the horror.

"Well answer then! It's the least you can do after
everything you're putting us through."
The room was deathly silent, and I began to wonder
if my brother and sisters were able to hear what was
being said. I knew they'd be trying their damnedest
to listen to every word and it was humiliating. I
hadn't considered the prospect of moving away, but
giving it thought now, I knew I couldn't stay at
home much longer.
I'd exposed my relationship with a family friend my
dad looked up to, and my mum probably had a
secret crush on. They had always hung on his every
word afterall.

"You're stuck between a rock and a hard place
now, aren't you?" he mocked. "It's all your own
doing, there's nobody to blame but yourself." He
turned his attention back to Bernie. "And you
should know better, your own daughter is a year
older than her. Why aren't you allowed to see your
daughter again?"

"It was a personal choice, I don't get on with her
mum, it's none of your business anyway so keep
your nose out. I'm trying to be the responsible adult
here and offer a roof over her head."

"I know exactly what your intentions are. That day she went missing and you came to look for her with us, you'd been with her hadn't you? Yet you still pretended to look for her with us." Bernie looked away.

"Say and think what you like, but I've done nothing wrong, if you think I have then call the police."

My parents must have known deep down that the situation was wrong, there was a huge fluorescent elephant in the room manically waving a red flag but they ignored it. An unhealthy 'relationship' had been developing for year's right under their own noses, and often in the next room.

"The only way this girl will be leaving the house with you, is in a body bag." Dad said with a smile, pleased to have come up with that sentence by himself.

"You're an absolute psychopath," said Bernie. "You have a draconian view of the world and one day you're going to end up a lonely old man."

"I don't care about your long words Bernie, but I know the two of you disgust where words fail me. You're not taking her anywhere."

"In two weeks you won't be able to stop her leaving." said Bernie.

"He's right," my mum interrupted.

That was it, my heart sank. It was at that moment I could feel my mum sever her ties that were barely there to begin with. It seemed everybody had

13

decided that I was going to leave home the day I turned sixteen.

"Let her move out," she said. "She'll soon come crawling back home. Let him see what kind of person she truly is and the heartbreak she causes. I want nothing more to do with her, she's no longer a part of this family. Let him have her."

It was these last four words that made me want to go back to the blameless beginning, the very beginning before I could even walk, a time when I would have been unaccountable for anything. As I began to ponder this, it hit me that my mum never really cared for me anyway. She had never really been there for me, never on my side, barely hugged or kissed me or showed affection like she did the others. I realised there was nothing left for me at this address.

I choked on the tears but spoke purposefully.

"Yes, I'm going to move out on my sixteenth birthday." I could barely believe my words as they dripped forcefully from my own mouth. I don't suppose I really knew what I was saying.

Mum said nothing, but scrunched her nose up and turned away. Dad looked shocked as though I'd put him in check mate; ending his gameplay.

"Well then, I guess there's nothing more to say," he turned to Bernie. "You stay away from my daughter until she's sixteen. And you," he pointed at me. "You're grounded. You'll be babysat by Beth, and she'll make sure you go to school. Everywhere you go from now on, people will be watching you, we'll tell them all what a dirty tart you are, and that you're running away with a paedo. You won't be able to show your face around here anymore."

He turned to Bernie.

"To think I let you into my house as a trusted friend, let you teach martial arts to my kids and give Moll piano lessons. You both make me sick."

Bernie got to his feet and he turned smugly to Dad.

"You, and your family are fucked up Jim." He said.

Then he left.

I decided to toughen up to cope with the criticism I received after the revelation. If I was going to be leaving home soon, I had to be emotionally prepared. The family pinned a calendar to the notice-board at home, to countdown and tick off every day that I remained in the house. It became a game to my siblings, who took it in turns to leave a smear with a red marker pen. They taunted me, given a free reign to treat me with as little respect as they pleased. My parents didn't speak to me either; they'd given up. I was somebody else's problem now.

Me and Bernie shared a mutual friend who was our go between whilst we were banned from contacting one another. It was a lad called John, who attended the same martial arts class and he was also the same age as me. We knew each other originally from the previous school we attended together. It was easy for Bernie to manipulate John into helping because he idolised Bernie and had a crush on me.

The day of my sixteenth birthday arrived and that morning I went to school as normal. There were no birthday cards, presents, or birthday wishes, and no desperate attempt to change my mind to stay. There was only dirty looks and name calling from the people I used to call family.

I needed John's mum to collect me and my belongings after school, and to let me wait at their house until Bernie could collect me. John's parents knew Bernie, and thought too that he was a decent intelligent fellow. I don't know whether John's mum was aware of an existing relationship, perhaps she'd have declined help if she'd have known.
I needed to ring John but didn't have enough money, my parents allowed me enough for my bus fare home, but that was all. I put some of my bus fare money in the pay phone at dinner time, knowing I could make one of the less popular kids replace it later.
The phone rang and I willed him to answer on every pause. Eventually, John's mum picked up the phone and I hung up, having no idea what to say to her. I felt incredibly desperate knowing I couldn't stay at home that evening, so I bit the bullet and put in the last of the bus fare money. Again it rang, and John's mum answered.
"Hello?"

16

"Hello, sorry to bother you but is John there please? I really need to speak to him."

"He's gone out dear, gone to look around a college for a course he's signed up for. He said you might call, Moll. He's asked me to collect you and your things from your house around four o'clock. Is that ok? Bernie will pick you up from ours around half past four. It's all been arranged."

I rested my head on the payphone and smiled, I had handled everything just like I'd expect an adult could, and I felt proud of myself. My deceptive, foolproof plan was in full swing and my parents knew nothing about it. I just had to face them now, knowing it wouldn't last beyond four o'clock. In a few hours - I'd be rid of them for good.

The line beeped, and the display flashed at me to insert more coins, so I quickly brought the call to a close.

"That's great thank you, I really appreciate all your help. See you at four o'clock."

"Okay, dear. See you then. Bye."

What was incredibly sad though, was the niggling thought in the back of my mind. If only my family had tried in a helpful way to convince me to stay then I might have done. If only they'd involved the police, this book would have ended after this first chapter. If only they'd recognised that this was abuse, and that I'd been the victim of Bernie's grooming for years.

But they didn't, (or chose not to). I guess that is
irrelevant now.

Chapter Two.

I sat on that damned bench for the last time, and waited for the bus to take me home as I fiddled with a ring on my finger. Bernie had driven over the day before during my dinner break. The school allowed us to go out during lunch, and he'd met me across the road in the car park of a public house.

It just wasn't the way I'd envisioned it when he proposed to me, pulling a cheap ring out of his pocket. The ring didn't fit, and he didn't have anything to say in particular.

It seemed very sudden, perhaps he thought it would guarantee me moving away with him. I even raised the subject, but he told me I was being paranoid and he started to become agitated.

So, a day before my sixteenth birthday, I was engaged to a man twenty four years older than myself. It offered me a little security but I was still dealing with the fallout on my own. I couldn't tell a soul about the engagement until I'd left home, of that he was adamant.

It was Thursday twenty ninth of October 1998. The next day would be a school day, I'd be waking up in another county, and the whole school would be gossiping about how I'd left home.

I watched my friends as they behaved like idiots, pushing each other into the road. I wasn't sure I'd miss them too much, and I couldn't tell them I was leaving. Bernie said it would just upset them, and I'd feel guilty about it afterwards.

With all the conflict at home, and my connection with Bernie, I'd well and truly cocked up my GCSE's. I didn't think there would be any point waiting about to sit them. The mock exams I took showed evidence that I'd be receiving some very high marks, it was the coursework that hindered me as I rarely did any.

My friends would come to and from school with folders of the stuff - I had none. I didn't get any help at home with it, my parents never showed any interest. It just never seemed important to anybody.

I did envy those friends in an odd way though, they had purpose and ambition. My only ambition it seemed, was to get as far away from there as possible, and my purpose? Well, I hadn't worked that part out, I merely existed day to day, looking for an exit.

In an hour or so, I'd be on a different journey. I'd already lived an awkward, short, lifetime of hell, which I contemplated on the journey home to give strength and further reason to my cause.

It was the first time I wished the bus didn't stop right outside my house. I knew they'd all be rubber-necking at the window, anticipating my return.

It was as though I'd walked into a stand-off as I crept through the front door. My mum and dad were waiting for me, and I had no doubts that they'd been thinking up things to say all day, running their scripts past each other and changing tactics. I had no comeback to whatever they'd throw at me. All I had was backbone and an iron will.

"So what's it going to be?" asked Dad, with a smug expression. "We've taken the liberty of packing your things already." He gestured to a pile of bin-liners that sat under the stairs. I didn't doubt for a second that my entire life could be squeezed into four bin-liners, and that they'd still contain as much air as they did. At least I knew their strategy, it was 'call my bluff', fortunately I had a plan of my own that they'd soon know about.

I told myself to stand my ground, to speak my purpose, that it would soon be over. However, I was frozen on the spot with my back against the front door for support.

I didn't say a word. It was a survival technique I'd learned living with that man, all he could do was shout at me and lose control of his own emotions. I was nothing like him.

Even in the midst of this very serious situation, he continued to play mind games with me. My mind was made up, and there would be nothing more they could say to convince me otherwise.

I'd picture perfected my new home with a tree in the garden, my new life without these games.

My silence had bought me a little time, I looked through the kitchen at the clock. John's mum should be arriving anytime, she did say 'around four o'clock.' Then doubt kicked in, what if she didn't turn up? What if Bernie changed his mind? What if the only knock that would come, would be that of the police? I started to panic inside.

21

I was about ready to drop the bombshell on them when my dad grasped my wrist and manhandled me into the kitchen. He pushed me into the worktop, and I hit my head on the cupboard above.

I panicked, what was I to do? Stand and fight back? They were my parents, I couldn't do that. I wouldn't give him the rise he was obviously looking for.

He pushed me hard into the cooker and my lower back burned and stung with pain.

He told me he was going to, 'knock my fucking lights out,' and my mum stood behind him watching.

"I'd slap you right around the face but you'd call social services wouldn't you? Because you're a spiteful little bitch." she said.

I wasn't sure whether she was actually asking for my permission to slap me, so I nodded my head.

"Yes, I'd call them straight out." I said.

I'd suddenly found my voice after sixteen years and it felt good. These people who had been given authority, responsibility, and rights over me since the day I was born, were just people to me now and I no longer wanted to take their crap.

I opened my mouth to inform them of my intentions but somebody knocked at the door.

I prayed and prayed harder that it would be John's mum. The timing would be perfect. *For once, please just let it go my way.* I prayed. The tension inside was unbearable, I was ready to snap in half.

They put on their happy masks, but not before my dad warned me that he was far from finished with me yet. It was John.

My mum answered the door and it was John who stood on the doorstep. He looked terrified but it was evident whose corner he was fighting.

"Are you ready Moll?" he asked me, as I lingered in the kitchen doorway.

My parents were speechless.

I moved carefully around them, conscious they could pounce on me like a pack of wild dogs any moment. I had a witness this time. John would call the police if they attacked me. This gave me a little confidence.

We each took two bin-liners, and John carried his to the car. I turned to my parents as I prepared to see them for the last time.

"I'm going now, I don't know when I'll see you again." I tightened my lips as they quivered, I was not going to cry.

"Don't bother," said Dad. You've done enough damage to this family." He couldn't look me in the face. I didn't even look at my mum, I couldn't bear to see that look of disappointment again. I didn't want to remember her like that. I didn't want to remember her at all.

I felt the heat on my face as it escaped the house, and I felt empowered to be standing on the other side of the threshold. I was standing outside with no curfew - I was free.

They were going to let me leave, just like that. No 'I love you's'- nothing.

I looked my dad square in the face, and for a moment, became the perfect mirror of his personality. I don't know where it came from but it had been trapped inside me for years.

"Not king of the fucking castle anymore are you?" I sneered, as I screwed up my nose and glared at him.

I took my bags and walked over to the car where John's mum was patiently waiting, seemingly oblivious to what was going on. My dad called out softly after me.

"We'll always be here if you need us."

I shook my head, *'just another mind game'*, I told myself as I climbed into the back of the car. I didn't look back as we pulled off. I hated them because they evoked such hate in me.

Bernie was supposed to be picking me up at half past four, I had all my hopes pinned on it. It was a cold October's evening, and the dark would soon be drawing in as I stood out in John's front garden, waiting.

His mum popped her head out now and again to see how I was getting on, she looked a little concerned and said they had a spare bedroom if I needed it, that I could stay for as long as I liked.

I wouldn't consider it at all, I'd committed my mind to moving to Peterborough. A change of strategy would have been too much to deal with and I'd likely have broken down. I'd pushed my emotional strength to the extreme already, so I pushed the doubts to the back of my mind.

A friend of mine who lived a couple of doors down walked across to me. I was a little overwhelmed at the sense of freedom I had. Normally, being stood about at this time of night with friends never happened without extreme consequences. The concern that my parents would soon be out looking for me was still lurking in the back of my mind because old habits die hard.

She offered me a room at her house for the night. Her parents were foster carers. I remember being very short with her and explained that Bernie was just running late. I couldn't tell her much else.

It unnerved me that everybody had given up hope, it was a time when mobile phones weren't as popular so I couldn't ring him to find out where he was.

I could barely feel my hands in the autumn freeze as Bernie's car rolled up at half past eight. I wanted to be angry, to shout, and to ask him where the hell he'd been, but I was in a very delicate situation. If I made him angry, (which I'd never seen before), he might well drive off, leaving me in a real predicament. Feelings of relief took over instead and I almost sobbed.

He seemed distracted and hurried me along.

"We'd better not hang about," he said, as he looked over his shoulder. "It'd be just like your parents to call the police."

"They don't know where I am and they don't know the address in Peterborough either." I said, as though I had it all figured out.

"Well let's not take that risk anyway." he said, as he roughly bundled my bin liners into the boot. I thanked John and his mum profusely as Bernie waited impatiently in the car. They wished me all the best with my new life. I got into Bernie's new Rover 214 and we headed towards the A47, leaving Leicestershire behind.

We didn't speak much during the drive, but as I looked out the window at the stars in the dark sky, Savage Garden began to play on the radio, 'To the Moon and Back,' It seemed quite fitting at the time. The most painful, heartfelt tears are the ones that run down the cheek when nobody is looking, and I noticed them as I caught my reflection in the window. Thoughts of my family lingered on my conscience. I pictured my siblings sat up in their rooms whilst my parents agonised downstairs, shouting and throwing things about the house, blaming each other - blaming me. Perhaps the opposite which would have been worst. Perhaps they were carrying on with their lives and had forgotten about me already. Maybe they did care in their own way; still they hadn't tried to stop me leaving. Even the rose tinted lenses couldn't fool my screaming heart. We drove past Perkins Engines as we came into Peterborough, I noticed how every building was an industrial sort until we drove a little further to somewhere that looked almost residential.

We passed a hotel, a shop, and a phone box until we came onto a road called 'Fengate'. There was a petrol station and a mobile home park.

We turned into that mobile home park and took the first left, until we came to a communal parking area.

"This is it," smiled Bernie. "This is our home." He studied my face for a reaction, he must have witnessed the exact moment my heart sank because it was too obvious to go unnoticed. I didn't want to appear ungrateful so I got out of the car.

"There's the tree I told you about," he said, pointing to something scrawny sticking out of the ground. It wasn't even a garden really, just rented earth between caravans. The tree was just an attempt to spruce up the shabby trailer park.

All of my life, I had been making fun of people that lived in caravans, now I'd be one of them - talk about karma.

As I walked up the broken steps, my second disappointment would be the front door that looked unsecure, after a quick rattle we were in.

Bernie turned on the lights and led me into a small sitting room, there were two dirty white plastic garden chairs which looked as though they'd been taken from the incomplete patio set outside. There was no television, only Bernie's computer, electric guitar, and a stereo that sat in the corner.

The carpet was sodden and smelled as though it was rotten right through, the walls were mouldy and painted an off-yellow colour. Suddenly I felt very foolish and I was sure I couldn't hide my disappointment.

"Come through and have a look at the kitchen," Bernie beamed, as he danced on the spot.
I took one step to the right and I was in the kitchen. It was equally as hideous as the living room, and I feared the mouldy theme would continue throughout the hell hole. Somehow, somebody had managed to squeeze a tiny table with two chairs into a space below the plastic window. The greasy brown cooker looked decades older than me, and there was no fridge.

"I've been using the cupboard under the sink to store milk, its cold enough," said Bernie. "You'll have to do the washing in the bath because we haven't got room for a washing machine. I've got a spinner for drying though, and there's a line out the back. You're a woman, I'm sure you'll be able to work out which washing powder you'll need to buy for hand washing."
I tried to pass it off as a minor inconvenience, sure I'd work it out eventually.
The bathroom was next on the left, painted a dull brown colour with a matching brown suite. The mouldy roller blind turned my stomach and I felt unclean just being in there.
The final blow came in the form of a double bedroom, this was when I understood the true nature of our 'relationship'.

I'd always been confused as to what the relationship really was. On the one hand, Bernie had treated me like a daughter and I saw him as a father, on the other hand, there had been sexual contact for a couple of years that I'd just gone along with it, not wanting to lose the one person in my life I felt I could rely upon, the one person who made me feel good about myself. I hadn't known any better.

The double bedroom to me, was a room of expectations, things I knew hardly anything about, things I'd not experienced until I met Bernie. The bed was covered half with a dusky pink sheet, the other half with a picnic blanket with a folded sleeping bag at the bottom. I was distracted by a sound from one of the cupboards that were built into the wardrobe.

"What's this?" I asked, as the buzzing got louder.

"It's an electric meter, coin operated. You put a pound in, you get electric. I thought you were supposed to be smart."

There was a small pile of coins inside the cupboard, I didn't know the value of money at all but guessed I'd be handling a lot more of it now.

Bernie showed me the last room in the caravan, a small porch that contained his filing cabinet and the spinner dryer. I hadn't seen anything like it before, there was a spout on the front that I imagined the water would drain out of, the old thing looked ancient and haunted.

You could fit one person in that room; two at a push.

"This is my smoking room," he smiled, as he rolled a cigarette in his tin. "So what's wrong with you? Don't you like the place? It's just I've paid money so you'd have somewhere to stay. You've barely said a word and to be honest, I'm starting to think you're being a little ungrateful, do you have any idea how much I've put on the line to bring you here?"

I didn't say a word, I just froze on the spot. It was the first time Bernie had ever raised his voice to me and it was because I'd upset him. I didn't mean to, I suppose in an odd way I missed my family and home regardless of how they treated me.

He went into the porch and slammed the door, it was pitch black in there and all I could make out was the amber glow of his roll up, and the whites of his eyes. At that moment I felt as though I was being stalked by a wild animal.

I don't care to go into detail other than to say that, by force, he took something irreplaceable from me that night, in that dirty, disgusting place I'd call home for the next two and a half years of my life.

Chapter Three.

I was born on the twenty nineth of October 1982, which today, makes me a 31 year old survivor of abuse. I was raised on a notorious council estate in Leicestershire. Living in a three bedroomed semi-detached house with six siblings (me being the middle child), and two parents. By todays standards, that would be considered over-crowding, though it was quite the norm back then.
My story starts from my earliest memories which I feel is important for you, the reader, to see how my stuation escalated. From neglected, child, to a child that became the victim of a much older man who groomed and abused me until the veil of naiivity lifted and I escaped.

The children howled with laughter and pointed as I stood in the corridor in a puddle of my own urine. It really wasn't my fault either, at five years old I didn't have great control over my bladder.
My dull, off-white knee high socks that had been handed down from my older sister, Beryl, and bleach boiled by my mother, were saturated. So were my new shoes with the little black flower. I was more concerned about those than the children laughing, it wasn't often I'd get something new that wasn't handed down and I knew they were ruined for good.
Mrs Floyd, my year one teacher, swept out of the classroom to where I stood and looked at me in disgust.

"You dirty Arab," she shouted, and the children sniggered from behind their cartons of break time milk.

I had asked to use the toilet which was in view at the end of the corridor, but was refused access from Mrs Floyd, who insisted I could wait until I'd finished my milk. That's when the little accident happened.

I dropped my carton on the floor as my teacher dragged me back into the classroom by my arm, as punishment; I was made to sit on a plastic carrier bag - on a chair in the corner, whilst she sent one of my classmates to find the caretaker.

I think I hated Mrs Floyd after that, I was certainly a little afraid of her. That playtime was spent rummaging through the lost property looking for something clean to wear, whilst I listened to the children playing outside. I could potentially reinvent myself in lost property as there were all kinds of thing in there, but I settled for a simple T-shirt and shorts.

I hoped the clean clothes would provide me with a second chance in the classroom, but it soon became apparent that nobody wanted to be my friend, or play with the girl that wet herself.

Most of the children knew each other since playschool and were already friends, I was the only one in my family who hadn't been to playschool, luckily I was well used to playing by myself.

Out in the corridor stood a wendy house I'd seen earlier, and I decided that it was quiet enough out there for me to play alone without being bothered. There was a pink plastic hairdryer on the side and I pretended to dry my long brown hair.

There was a sudden thud at the door and the house shook a little, I thought nothing of it and resumed play. Then another thud, which knocked the cereal cartons off the shelf.

I leaned out of the window to see where the banging was coming from, where I saw some of the children piling large plastic blocks against the door under the instruction of a little girl with blonde pigtails. They sat on the blocks laughing as I tried to push the door open against them.

"You have to stay in there because you smell like wee," said the little blonde girl.

I shouted for Mrs Floyd and the children quickly moved away from the door, which meant I could escape and tell the teacher.

"They locked me in the wendy house," I sobbed at my teachers' desk side.

"Don't be so silly, there are no locks on the door. It was probably just stuck."

"But they *did* lock me in there."

Mrs Floyd looked over her glasses a me.

"Nobody likes a tattle tale, why don't you go and play somewhere else on your own if you can't play with the others."

I stomped out of the classroom feeling angry and frustrated, and I dragged myself back over to the wendy house to resume play. The blonde haired girl was now playing with the hair dryer and she didn't look as though she intended to share.

"You can't come in here, you stink." She said.
I was surprised by her audacity, and thought the teacher would have at least come out to check on us, but she didn't.
I ignored her and reached for the hairdryer, but she snatched it back and pushed me towards the door.

"Get out!" she shouted.
I hoped the teacher would come running out and catch her in the act but it never happened.
She pushed me again and I fell out the door onto the blocks where the children were playing, they laughed at me again. Then something snapped inside me.
I got to my feet and pushed the door open before the girl could protest. I hoisted her out of the chair by her pigtails and slammed the plastic wendy house door repeatedly on her head.
Mrs Floyd came screaming out and tore me off the girl who was hysterical.
She comforted her and I was banned from playing with anything else for the rest of the day.
This was my first memory of school.

Chapter Four.

Time soon slipped past and the summer holidays were over, I'd be in year two this time around. I'd managed to survive a full year in Mrs Floyd's classroom. I'd even managed to make a couple of friends.

That morning, I skipped to school swinging my blue Puddle Lane lunchbox, stopping momentarily to watch the blackbirds suck worms from the ground. It was a cool crisp morning and the path was dusted with a gentle frost.

"Hurry up or you'll be late for school," said my mum sternly. "You're an impossible child, you'll make us all late."

My older sister Beryl had told me about Mrs Biggins, who would be my new teacher. Apparently she was a witch who locked children in her broom cupboard, (where I suppose she kept her broomstick).

My stomach near fluttered away as the bell rang, and I lined up in the bustling playground. Mrs Biggins stood in front of us, she didn't look like a stereotypical witch to me, she was a petite lady in her early fifties perhaps, she dressed conservatively, had short curly grey hair and large bifocal glasses.

It was half way through the first lesson of the day that I decided she absolutely wasn't a witch and that I rather liked her. Her face lit up when she smiled and she paid an equal amount of attention to each of us.

It was the best week of school I remember to this day, Mrs Biggins even taught me how to tell the time. She read stories to us and helped me when I struggled with reading. She made learning fun.

At the end of the week, my mum was called into school. I tried frantically to recall anything I might have done wrong. Normally when I came to enjoy myself, things would take a turn for the worst and it seemed this occasion was no different. I spent the whole of the day on edge, unable to enjoy anything as the little waves of adrenaline unnerved my stomach.

When my mum arrived at the end of the day, Mrs Biggins took her to one side and expressed concern with my eyesight.

"She's struggling to read from the chalkboard," I heard her say. "I think she needs glasses before she starts to miss out on things."

It was true, but the subject had never been raised before, my eyesight had been terrible for as long as I could remember.

"Is that all?" asked my mum. "What about her behaviour?"

"Well no actually," said my teacher. "Her behaviour has been fine, but she isn't wearing any knickers today. Did you send her school without them?"

"Of course not," said my mum, raising her voice. I tugged on Mrs Biggins jumper until she bent down to let me whisper in her ear.

"Oh I see," she giggled, "wait here, I'll be back in a minute."

My mum looked at me and rolled her eyes.

"You're impossible." she said.

I ignored her and watched Mrs Biggins, as she walked back past the window carrying my knickers at the end of a wooden ruler. I'd lost them getting changed for swimming that morning.

"Don't worry," she smiled reassuringly, "this happens more often than you think."

She took a plastic bag from her coat, put them inside and handed them to my mum who made me carry them home.

It was around a week later when I got my first pair of glasses, the optician said he didn't know how I'd coped without them as my prescription was terrible. I was able to choose my own glasses too, they were pink with little flowers on. He showed me a case which snapped shut and had a pale pink lining. I really wanted it but wouldn't push the matter in case my mum couldn't afford it. I didn't want to put her in an awkward situation because I knew I'd suffer for it later when she told my dad. To my delight, the case was included with the glasses and I was very happy with them.

I absolutely loved being able to see properly and not bump into things, though I felt a little anxious wearing them for the first time at school incase people laughed. Mrs Biggins made a point of telling everyone how pretty I looked with my new glasses, and my nerves were soon eased. She helped to clean them when they got 'fingerprinty'. She was much like the grandma I wished for and nothing like my own.

It was dinner time, and I queued with my Puddle Lane sandwich box waiting to be seated. I remember the smell of the freshly polished wood flooring, and the P.E apparatus that folded flat against the wall. The kitchen clattered with pots and pans which echoed about the place as the dinner ladies laughed. A space became available for me to eat, though most of the children were in the years above me. I opened my sandwich box and was astounded to discover its contents. It was a par frozen pizza, evident from the little dusting of ice that sat on the cheese. I closed it quickly and sat silently waiting for the older children to finish their hot meals. The chairs which soon became vacant were quickly filled with new faces, as the staff pressed to get though dinner time as quickly as they could. I daren't open my sandwich box knowing people would laugh.

My dithering had attracted the attention of a dinner lady who moved me outside the hall, (where the disruptive children were seated), because they needed to put the tables and chairs away. She asked me why I wasn't eating my lunch and I showed her the frozen pizza.

"I think it needs a bit longer to defrost," I told her as I poked at it. She told me to sit still for a moment whilst she went back into the kitchen.

One of the dinner ladies, Mrs Patton, who I liked for her smiling dimples, came from the kitchen. Her brown crescent shaped eyes were red and puffy and it looked like she'd been crying.

"Are you okay Mrs Patton?" I asked.

"Yes dear," she smiled, as she placed a tray of hot food on the table in front of me. "Eat up, I know it isn't much but dinner time is almost over and it's all that was left."

She tossed the pizza into a rubbish bag and took away my sandwich box whilst I ate one of the best meals I'd had for a long time. My blue puddle lane box came back shiny as the day it was bought and Mrs Patton had cleaned all the mould that was growing inside it. She ruffled my hair and cleaned the fingerprints from my new glasses as the bell rang. She told me to go back to the classroom before I made myself late.

As she walked back into the kitchen, I overheard her talking to the others, she said something about reporting it to the head-teacher and it scared me. I wondered if my parents would get the bill for the meal. I imagined how they'd rant at me for not appreciating what I'd been given.

I heard nothing from the head-teacher that afternoon but it loomed over my head like a black cloud. I was in a permanent state of heightened anxiety, and each time somebody walked through the classroom door, I'd feel that familiar wave of nausea that made me uncomfortable in my own skin.

I walked home dragging my feet as my sister, Beryl, teased me about my glasses. She called me 'four eyes', 'Biggles', and anything else her tiny mind could muster up.

The tarmac glistened as it warmed in the heat, and I ran up the driveway noting my father's friend, Derrick, had parked his car on the drive. I was relieved as my dad rarely shouted at me if people were there. I never did like Derrick, there was something about him that made my skin crawl.

I played in the back room with my sisters little mermaid doll, she never appreciated her toys and the broken ones often got passed on to me when they were worn and no longer loved. I'd built up quite a good collection of things unwanted.

I could hear my dad and Derrick giggling in the living room, there was a hatch-way where a door once used to be. Every time his friends came over, they'd chain smoke underneath the yellow nicotine stained ceiling.

Then I heard him call my name and my heart almost dropped though the floor. My sister, Beth, looked smugly at me, and that familiar dizziness and cold sweat returned as I shuffled past the hatch-way clutching the mermaid doll.

"Moll's going to get in trouble," she sang.

I walked through the hallway and stopped for a moment outside the living room door. A hundred thoughts charged through my mind at that point, and I tried to recall anything I might have done. The only incident I could think of was the one with the

40

cold pizza, and it occurred to me that the head-teacher may have called home. As I slowly opened the door, I mentally scrambled about, trying to come up with an excuse. I decided to say my frozen pizza had fallen onto the floor which was why I couldn't eat it.

"Don't look so worried, you're not in trouble" he said. "We just wanted to see what your new glasses look like."
I think I may have smiled a little at that point, it wasn't often that the focus of attention was entirely on me.

"Oh, they look very special don't they Jim?" said Derrick, in his slimy, greasy voice. He wore glasses himself but they were bifocals which made his wandering eyes appear much bigger than they were. I'd never been one to accept compliments, somehow they always seemed fake and insincere.

"Are you going to say thank you to Derrick or just stand there?" he asked me.

"Thank you Derrick," I said, knowing I'd have to before it escalated. Now wasn't the time to let the awkward silence devour me.

"Go and give him a hug then," he said, with a smile.
I stood frozen to the spot, hugging Derrick was absolutely the last thing I wanted to do. I didn't feel comfortable embracing my own parents in such a manner, I didn't want to be anywhere near this slimy stranger.

"But I don't want to," I said, as tears began to glaze my eyes, hoping my eyes didn't look bigger in my new glasses because they'd see the tears.

"Don't be such a silly little cow and give Derrick a hug before he gets offended, because if he does, you'll be in trouble."

I walked over to Derrick slowly, avoiding eye contact, he hoisted me up onto his knee and squeezed me tight. I could smell the stale tobacco on his breath as he laughed. I clung to the mermaid doll and thought about that instead. I thought of the adventures I could be having under the sea if I could be a real mermaid and not an unwanted toy.

"You look very sexy in your new glasses," laughed my dad, in the way he joked about to make Derrick snigger. I freed myself from Derrick's grasp and jumped down, not knowing where to look in the room as they both appeared to be studying my reaction.

"You could be our sexetary," he sniggered. "Would you like that?"

I knew what a secretary was but not a 'sexetary', even at six years old I considered it to be a bad, dirty word.

I didn't say a word, but stood staring at the floor for a little while before he sent me back to play in the next room. They howled with laughter as I quietly closed the door.

I went up to my bedroom that I shared with my five sisters and looked out of the window at the kids playing in the street. It would be dark before my

42

mum would be back from work, but I knew better than to wait for her as I used to. I'd sit on the windowsill and wait to see her shadow disturb the street-lit pavement.

I hoped one day that she'd spend time with me, and maybe she might even enjoy my company. She was always too busy or too tired, and the others pushed harder for her affection until I gave up trying.

I took my glasses off and put them in the pink case I used to love, as it snapped shut, I told myself that would be the last time I'd ever wear them in case other people looked at me in the way my dad and Derrick had.

I curled up on my side of the bed and drifted off to sleep to the sound of laughter downstairs. I slept away many evenings like this because it passed the time away and nobody seemed to notice. I'd go many evenings without dinner because my dad wouldn't wake me up.

My mum was eventually told that I was sleeping a lot, and my dad said it was because I thought I was better than everybody else in the house. That made me an easy target for my siblings, as they believed every word he said, and blamed every little thing on me from then on.

My glasses ended up stuffed underneath my bed at the very back and I continued to struggle with my class work. Eventually, Mrs Biggins decided, (after many false promises to bring my glasses back into school), that I was unwilling to help myself and she didn't show me as much attention towards the end of the school year. That relationship ended as quick as it had started.

My dad drank a lot of tea, he almost liked it as much as cigarettes. He had his own cup which we weren't allowed to wash, despite the thick brown staining around the inside. He thought it added character to the taste. He'd even drink it cold when it had been left stewing for hours.
My mum used to take him a cup upstairs when he'd be having his daily bath, but as she was working longer hours, she was no longer able to most days.

I stood washing up in the kitchen one day, and my dad came in to put the kettle on. He was routing through a large pile of clean washing on the kitchen table as he was going in the bath. He 'accidentally' dropped a pair of black satin briefs onto the floor, I looked down as I felt them bush my leg. They had a gold zip that ran up over the crotch area.

"Oops, sorry, I wasn't looking for those," he laughed, as he bent down to pick them up. "These are your mum's favourites, she loves it when I wear them but they look a little bit funny with the zip. Do you know what it's for?"
I shook my head quickly and started to scrub at a badly stained pan, hoping he'd leave the conversation there - which he did.

"I'm going in the bath in a minute, in about fifteen minutes, will you make a new pot of tea? Just bring it up and don't worry about knocking."

44

Then he left the kitchen taking his satin briefs with him.

I was horrified, something felt very wrong about the situation but I knew if I didn't take his tea up then he'd punish me with his belt or slipper like he often did.

I looked at the clock and tried to remember what Mrs Biggins had taught me about time, and I found where fifteen minutes would be.

I barely remember making the tea, but know I would have put three sugars in it even on autopilot. The last telling off I got was because I put too much sugar in and it ended with the tea being wasted. I was smacked so hard on my leg that I couldn't sit down at school.

When I reached the bathroom at the top of the stairs, such was my desire not to progress a step further, that I considered throwing myself back down to avoid seeing my dad in the bath.

As I opened the door, the first thing I noticed was the lack of scent, which meant he'd not used bubble bath and every part of him would be on full display. The air was moist and I desperately tried not to inhale even a single breath of it, because his perspiration was likely to have contaminated the air. He sat in a fairly shallow bath but didn't bother to cover his modesty which was in plain view. It seemed almost as though he enjoyed watching my eyes dart about the bathroom, looking for a safe place for them to settle.

"Can you bring it over here please before it goes cold?" he asked brazenly, as though the situation was entirely normal.

"It's bloody cold!" my dad spat it out into the bath after taking a sip.

"But I thought you liked cold tea?" I said.

"I do, but not when I'm in the bath. It's because you're too damn lazy to make a new pot of tea, isn't it? You don't give a damn about anybody but yourself in this house."

I didn't say anything, I just looked at the floor which was slowly flooding as his movements became more animated.

"Just get out," he said. "I'm disappointed with you yet again. I give you one important job and you can't even get that right. You're not part of this family."

He picked up a wet towel and threw it in my face. I moved downstairs as quickly as I could.

About an hour later I could hear my dad moving about. The stairs creaked as he came down and I knew he'd come in, I had no time to go into the back room where the others were playing, I even thought about climbing through the hatchway into the next room to avoid a conversation with him. He came through the door with just a towel wrapped loosely around his waist and he strode across the living room to his chair. He sat with his legs open wide enough to make someone feel uncomfortable. I was watching 'You've Been Framed', a popular TV show where people send in their own funny home videos, if they were shown, there was a prize of £250. My dad always found it hilarious and would sometimes laugh until he cried. Often he'd still be hysterical long after everybody else had stopped.

He started talking about his own ideas for a home video as he wanted the £250 for a new pair of binoculars. My sisters came in to watch the show too.

My dad had built a bar with an integrated fish tank that you could walk behind to stand at the counter. I had memories of watching him build it when I was younger. I remember eating a slice of watermelon when he was sawing the wood, disappointed with the seeds that were inside the melon. 'If you eat the seeds, a watermelon will grow out of your bum,' he used to say to me. That thought alone terrified me as watermelons are quite massive.

Without warning, he stood up and the towel fell from his waist. He giggled as he ran behind the bar and said that it was a shame we didn't have the video camera to hand, as we could have sent the clip in.

Everyone in the room thought it was hilarious but my stomach churned over inside.

Chapter Five.

My eighth birthday soon came about which brought with it, that odd birthday immunity. When somebody had a birthday in our house, everyone would be nice to them and any grievance would be put off until the next day.

I can't recall exactly what gifts I received, but vividly remember a small box that my dad handed me. It was blue with a velvet lining, and in the centre sat a small heart shaped silver ring. It was the first time I'd ever known him to acknowledge my birthday so today seemed extra special.

It was evidently bought from a well-known catalogue store on the High Street, and my sister, Beryl, would later trawl though the catalogue to discover it cost under £5. She would tease me about it but I didn't care how much it cost because it belonged to me and nobody else. It would become the first and last piece of jewellery I'd ever want to wear.

I'd come home from school every day and the ring would come out of the box and go on my finger. If I ever forgot, (which didn't happen often), my dad would remind me.

I'd come home from school each day and put the ring on, taking it off at bedtime as it became routine. One particular night in bed, I could hear my dad moving about downstairs, it was late but because he slept during the day as he was quite nocturnal.

I heard his footsteps on the stairs, slow and quiet. He opened the bedroom door and stood looking at me for some time, before turning away and going to the bathroom. I don't understand why he did it so often and I don't remember why it used to scare me to death, but I used to pretend I was asleep.

I was different to my siblings, I wouldn't let him break my spirit. Every time he'd keep me up until silly o'clock in the morning, sat on that chair in the middle of the living room, trying to break a confession from me for something I hadn't done, I'd stick to my word. It would often be a smack or the slipper for me. One day he hit me so hard that I couldn't sit properly at school. I was examined by the school nurse and my mum was called in. It was never much fun having to strip down to your vest and pants, even though she was no stranger to me anymore.

I remember after my mum left that day, I had to go back into assembly, I sat and cried for her. The teacher moved me next to the piano at the front as the school sang 'Morning Has Broken."

I returned home from school that day and went upstairs to put my ring on. I opened the little blue box and slipped it onto my finger but something wasn't right.

I felt a pinch on the back of my finger and turned my hand over to discover the ring looked as though it had been cut straight down the back, split in half on the band.

It nearly put me on the floor. I was worried my dad would find out.

I'd been so gentle and careful with it, I knew that it definitely wasn't in that condition when I put it back.

I couldn't tell him about it because I knew he'd go up the wall, so I just put it on and went downstairs, hoping the conversation would never come up.

I was conscious of the pinching all evening. I couldn't enjoy TV or my dinner because it bothered me so much. It was the first evening my dad hadn't mentioned the ring, in fact, he barely registered I was there at all.

The next day I was so pleased to not be wearing the ring to school. I knew my dad would be in bed all day and unlikely to find where I'd hidden it inside my pillowcase.

I couldn't concentrate on anything except that damn ring and its phantom pinch. I imagined my dad going through my things and coming across it. I worried about a confrontation at home. Maybe he'd search my room because he saw I was acting strange the previous evening.

When I did get home, he said nothing to me. My mum came home late and went straight to bed so I didn't get to speak so much as a word to her. I wanted to tell her about the ring but she didn't have the time.

I was last up to bed again that night, my dad wanted to talk about dinosaurs because he thought I was interested in them. It was my own doing really.

We'd been to the museum on one rare family outing and I saw a box of dinosaurs I wanted. I was a typical child and wanted everything even though I didn't know what half the stuff was.

To my amazement, they bought me the box of dinosaurs and from then on, I had to make them believe I was really interested in them so I didn't get told off.

It was then that Dad raised the matter of the absent ring on my finger. I'd been so anxious that he'd find out it was somehow broken, that I'd completely forgotten to put it on.

I went upstairs to my room and stuck my hand into my pillowcase to find it - it wasn't there.

I opened the dressing table where it was normally kept and it was right there, back in its box.

I felt sick to the stomach, I knew I hadn't imagined it and it was in a place where I hadn't left it. To make matters worse, when I put the ring on, there was no split at the back!

I did not want to go back downstairs at all. I was sure he'd mention something about it. He must have known it was broken, yet I couldn't explain how it had turned up somewhere else in one piece. I certainly hadn't dreamt it, I was well used to these mind games he played.

I looked at my sister's fast asleep in their beds, I so desperately wanted to be one of them at that moment. I sometimes wondered if they were actually awake and thanking their lucky stars they weren't in my shoes.

51

I walked slowly downstairs, hoping my dad would have fallen asleep and stood awkwardly in the doorway until he spotted me and told me to sit back down. He wanted to continue the conversation about dinosaurs whilst he watched a lady dance naked around a pole on television to some sleazy music.

I hated it when he put these programs on in front of me. I never knew where to look and I always felt he was watching me for a reaction.

He'd sit with his eyes fixed on the TV, then he'd talk to me about dinosaurs and a long pause would come whilst he watched the woman again. I often wondered what he was thinking during these moments, because it wasn't the first time it had happened.

I felt so awkward that I made my excuses to go to bed. He asked me to put the dog out in the garden first so that it could do its business underneath the weeping willow tree.

When I came back in, he was very short with me and told me to go to bed if I didn't want to talk to him.

It was two o'clock in the morning and I had to be up for school in the morning.

I crept up to bed and fell asleep feeling very isolated indeed.

I never can recall how I lost that ring, but it was never spoken of again.

Chapter Six.

My older sister Beryl had signed up to a modelling agency which made my parents very proud. They'd shower her with new clothes every week, and my dad would help to build her portfolio by taking, (looking back now as an adult) what were quite risqué shots of her in the back garden. She was often wearing very little.

I despised her smugness, and the way she'd tell me that I'd never be a model because I wasn't pretty enough. Freckles weren't 'in' apparently. Also, I was too much of a tomboy, (which I owed to my brother's hand me downs), and because I was covered in scabs, as I used to pick at my skin out of anxiety when my mum wasn't there.

My face and arms were covered in them, and my parents would always make a point of telling me how ugly it made me look.

I wasn't too bothered because I didn't want to be a model, I wanted to be a scientist which I felt was a much more respectable job. It wouldn't really matter if I was covered in scabs and scars.

I was never jealous of the way Beryl looked, because quite frankly, she was hideous, but more of the attention she was given and the nice clothes she was bought. She had a huge nose and I called her 'Concorde' and duck every time she'd turn around.

Because of her stuck up attitude, I often hid her clothes when she needed them for modelling. My favourite spot where I knew she'd never find them was in my brother's pillowcase, and in her own duvet. I was always the first suspect, but I enjoyed watching her panic as she shouted at me, desperately trying to find them whilst her freshly made up face and hair dripped with sweat and fell out of place.

When my hiding places were discovered and the bruising from my dad's slipper had faded away, I'd put her clothes in my school bag and hide them in my locker at school where I knew she'd absolutely never be able to gain access.

Each Wednesday, one of us would get to go with Mum to the city in the evening to take Beryl to one of her modelling sessions. Today it would be my turn.

I'd heard stories from the others who had been before, how they'd secretly eaten out at a well-known fast food establishment that our father had forbidden us to use because he'd heard rumours that they sponsored the IRA. He was well into his conspiracy theories, likely because they made him feel he was still part of society, without the responsibility that came with it. Today it was my turn to join the rebellious eaters club and I was most excited.

We caught the double decker bus, and I convinced them to sit upstairs, (mainly by walking up the steps anyway). Mum stared lovingly at Beryl who was the apple of her eye, whilst I pulled faces in the mirror that the driver uses to see what was going on upstairs. I looked out of the window for the majority of the journey, whilst they chatted about Beryl's plans for super stardom.

"I want to start in magazines first and then maybe get into television," said Beryl.

We got off at the bus station and the driver smiled at me as I hopped off. Beryl got dropped off at her vanity building. Mum didn't take me inside which she thought was in Beryl's best interest because of my scabs and scars. Her skin was greasy and riddled with acne but it didn't stop her looking down her big concorde nose at me.

When we left, Mum was more vacant than usual. I didn't get the meal I'd been so looking forward to, though I did get a doughnut and a drink.

We reached a pay phone and she made a phone-call to Dad as she normally did to let him know we'd got there okay. They had a small but heated exchange and she slammed the receiver down.

I followed quickly behind her as she stormed off back in the direction of the bus station, where we sat on some fold down seats, clock watching until it was time to pick Beryl up.

"You know," she started, "if it wasn't for you lot, we wouldn't have arguments like this." she paused. "If it wasn't for you kids, I'd leave your father and be happy."

I remember feeling a little crushed as the burden of adult problems was placed upon my shoulders. I didn't know what to say, so I sat in silence watching the clock tick by.

Mum barely spoke until it was time to pick Beryl up from twenty minutes walk away. I was glad to stretch my feet.

The outing was nowhere near as exciting as I'd expected, and I felt a little deflated as I walked alongside my mum, not daring to try holding her hand.

"You know how you came into this world don't you?"

I assumed she was speaking to me and was thankful for the conversation, I shook my head.

"No?"

"It's a funny story really. Want to hear it?"

"Yes," I smiled, because now it was all about me and I was getting the attention from her that I so desperately craved.

"Well, it all started when my dad – your granddad, died. You never got the chance to meet him because he died before you were born. Your Nana was in a right state for a long time afterwards so we had her move in with us. It was fine to begin with and we'd not long had your brother. Your Nana had her own ideas about the way we should be bringing Alex up and we didn't agree with her interfering."

I listened intently, waiting for the part where it would become all about me.

"Anyway, after we fell out, she locked herself in the bedroom and refused to come out. We left trays of food outside the door but she refused to eat, like she was on some kind of hunger strike. We were getting worried about her until your father caught her shimmying down the drainpipe one evening. It turned out that she'd been sneaking off to the bingo every evening for her dinner. We were so cross when we found out and we'd had enough of her interfering so decided she had to go."

I giggled a little, I'd never had a relationship with my Nana because she never seemed to like me, but the imagery of her sneaking out the house made me laugh.

"That's why we had you. Because then there would no longer be space for her and she'd have to move out. Funny though, I get on better with her since she moved out."

She smiled at me and I smiled back as I choked the tears away, it was dark so she couldn't see my true reaction.

At least I understood now why Nana had always disliked me and treated me differently to the others. She'd always 'forget' to buy me presents at Christmas, whilst everyone else got teddy bears and watches. When she'd be called upon to babysit, I'd play behind the sofa while she watched Coronation Street. The whiny melody of the theme tune still makes my skin crawl when I hear it and I'll always remember that cat that slinked along the wall during the intro. Nana would always be telling me to play quieter else she'd smash my toys to pieces and tell my mum that I was responsible. I didn't mind being behind the sofa so much because at least I didn't have to look at her haggard, hateful, old face.

We reached the modelling agency and Beryl was waiting for us outside in a fit of hysterical tears. The reason unfolded on the walk back to the bus station, me lagging behind from the weight of my heavy heart, and my mum comforting Beryl. As we waited for our bus, she continued to tell us how the evening had been like an exam and how they'd been graded on the various things models have to do. Things like walking down the catwalk while maintaining the correct posture, she was also graded on her physical appearance and attire. She'd been given an 'A' for posture and grace which Mum reassured her was an excellent grade. She scored a 'B' for attire and a 'C minus' for her face which was the reason for her inconsolable crying.

"It's the worst thing in the world," she sobbed.

"Worse than war, and those children starving in Africa?" I asked, genuinely interested in her response.

My heart felt a little lighter and Beryl must have seen it written across my face because she scowled and accused me of smirking which I apparently did quite a lot.

The journey home was relatively peaceful apart from the sound of Beryl's crocodile tears and my mum's comforting words.

I wished we'd caught the same double decker bus home because I felt like I really needed to see somebody smile at me again.

Chapter Seven.

Amy was late to call for me that morning. She'd normally be at my house by eight o'clock, so I figured she was probably off sick or bunking off, so I left without her.

I stepped out into the cold grey morning and shivered as the remaining fog spattered my face like a light rain shower.

I was anxious at the prospect of having to walk past Mrs Arnold's house alone, me and Amy had trodden on her flowerbeds the previous week. Not for any particular reason other than we were silly, immature twelve year olds.

There was an odd sensation looming in the air that day which I could not place my finger on, other than to say that things just felt *wrong*.

Nobody was about as my footsteps echoed on the lonely pavement where crowds of children would normally gather as they walked to school.

I walked quickly past Mrs Arnold's house with my head down like a coward until I heard a thud of footsteps becoming louder behind me. I spun around expecting Mrs Arnold, but it was Amy.

"Hurry up else you'll make me late again." I shouted.

She doubled over when she reached me and tried to catch her breath as she held up one hand.

"I didn't think you'd be in school today," she panted. "Haven't you heard what happened last night?"

"No?" I said, thinking that if it was a reason for not being in school then I very much wanted to hear about it.

"It's Darren, I can't believe you haven't heard, didn't you see the police cars and ambulance go down our road last night?"

I shook my head.

"He hung himself at the golf course, they found him last night. We went down there to see what was going on but they'd cleared everything up by then so we couldn't see anything."

I felt as though I'd taken a blow to the stomach and had the wind knocked out of me, I think I was in shock.

I'd been forced into joining the St. Johns Ambulance some years ago, I didn't enjoy it and regarded it as social suicide. We learned all about shock there, and this was it.

"What?" I managed to slur, becoming aware of my feet that felt as though they were setting in concrete. I'd heard her clearly enough, but my brain couldn't process the information.

"He's dead, Jesus I can't believe you didn't know about it, everyone on our road has known for hours." She put her hands around her throat, made a choking sound and laughed.

She'd always been an immature idiot but at that moment, I realised I had nothing in common with her at all and I wanted her out of my sight before I scratched her eyes out.

Darren was my childhood friend, I'd known him since I first started school, we'd not hung out as much these past few years because he was in the year above me and we had very different friends. I had mainly idiot friends like Amy that would take a piece of devastating news like this, and turn it into idle gossip for laughs.

"Look Amy, just go away." I said, with a tremble in my voice.

"I didn't think you talked to Darren anymore, I can't see why you're so bothered."

"Seriously, just go away." I said again.
She shrugged her shoulders and turned on her heels to walk to school with the red face of rejection.

I didn't know which way to turn, I wanted to bury my head somewhere as the tears settled on my water line, deciding whether to drip or torment my lashes. I was closer to home than I was to school and could have turned and gone back at any point. I needed an adult.
My mum would be at work, and my dad would still be in bed and would be angry if I woke him. I'd be a burden to them if it turned up so I decided to go to school instead. My dad would probably call me a liar anyway and say I was attention seeking. The more I thought about it, the more it occurred to me that Amy may well be lying, she was a serial joker but she had a spiteful streak in her too, this would be stepping way over the line.

I can't recall how long I stood in the street but Mrs Arnold came out to scold me about the flowers. She stopped dead when she saw me.

"Good god child, whatever is the matter? You look white as a sheet."

I suppose I was in a daze as I looked at her.

"I'm sorry about the flowers," I mumbled, as I turned and made my way to school.

The gates were crowded when I arrived, I scoured the bike hut for Darren's bike as I passed, it was normally propped up in an arrogant fashion against someone else's bike.

It wasn't there.

I continued gingerly into a school that was swarming with, what I would later learn to be counsellors. People were sitting on the floor crying, the whole place had become chaotic. The teachers had slackened their ties a little, the order seemed unbalanced somewhat. Then I felt in my heart that it was true.

By the time I reached my classroom, we were hoisted off into an assembly in the lecture theatre. There were more counsellors there and some very sombre looking teachers.

"I have some very sad news," began our head-teacher. "Yesterday, a pupil here many of you know very well, took his own life."

Darren's teacher, Mr Thompson scoured the room, making eye contact with his class, then he briefly looked at me. I don't know what sort of reaction he was looking for but I don't think I gave him any.

"As you will already have noticed, we have many counsellors in our school today and they'll be available to anybody who needs them."
My stomach churned and twisted and I wanted to go home. It was too much, the sound of children crying and moaning, trying best to deal with the tragedy. My throat felt as though it was shrinking as the lump grew bigger and it hurt to try and swallow it down.
To me, the lecture theatre had always been an overbearing, almost intimidating place to be but in light of today, it suddenly seemed a lot smaller, and the acoustics were practically non-existent. The ceiling appeared to be lower and the walls as though they'd moved in to unite us closer in our grief. It was as though those very walls were absorbing every emotion and projecting it right back at us as we expressed our various degrees of grief, and for some, perhaps even guilt.
I can't remember much of what was said after that, something about a memorial service that would be held on the day of Darren's funeral once they could determine the date. I looked over to Amy, her eyes reddened and puffy were full of remorse. I forgave her instantly, her crime seemed insignificant now. They mentioned no cause of death besides stating he took his own life. I suppose they were just shielding us from the grisly truth but it left a lot of questions unanswered for some. As morbid as it may sound, it was likely I thought, that they didn't want to say the word 'suicide' at the risk of glamorising it.

We went back to our classrooms in silence, the counselling sessions were in full swing. I thought some of the children were probably there to skip lessons, but I suppose that could have been the cynic in me.

I sat at my desk with my head in my hands and people left me alone. I'd grown a reputation for unpredictable behaviour and lashing out which was probably the reason.

I didn't go to see the counsellor myself, I couldn't see how their long words and awkward silences could bring me relief. They couldn't bring Darren back, they couldn't turn back the clock and bring back yesterday. A counsellor seemed rather pointless so I continued the day in my angry, zombie state.

At lunchtime, I grew sick and tired of people talking about it in such a flippant manner. Everywhere I went it was; 'Darren this, Darren that,' until I could no longer bear it.

It was only days ago we stood yards away from where I was now stood. We were in the dinner queue and he announced to everybody within earshot that their pubic hair was the same length of the hair on their arms. Shortly before stuffing a cake into my pocket and framing me for the crime. That was his sense of humour, his jokes were often vile and uninhibited but incredibly funny. He was the clown and now we were all in mourning for him.

I walked over to the office where the school photos hung on the wall, Darren stood in the back row with his head down, the only person whose face you couldn't see. That was another of his jokes and he'd it immortalised in the school reception area.

I can't recall exactly what was going on in my head when I punched that photo off the wall, I don't remember clenching my fist but I remember how everything seemed to just stop, even the despair subsided. The moment the photo smashed on the ground, the noise started again.

The receptionist came out from the office and the deputy head came screaming around the corner. They didn't yell but just looked at me standing over the crime scene.

I wanted to experience real feelings again, I wanted to feel fear, I wanted to be shouted at – punished even. I just wanted to make sense of the way I felt inside, to justify the uncontrollable rage I felt but I didn't know how.

The deputy head, Mr Law, took me into his office and the receptionist made me a cup of tea as I slumped into an armchair, I knew the drill, I'd been in that office enough times.

"I understand you're going to be feeling a plethora of emotions for some time to come, however nothing justifies vandalising school property. I know it may seem harsh right now but in hindsight, there are children and staff that may have wanted to look at that picture too." He smiled a little. "Lord knows we're all feeling angry because we don't understand why it happened. Why somebody would take their own life like that, what you're feeling is very normal. I know members of staff here feel very similar to the way you do, I'm not saying they know exactly what you're going through because that would be condescending and unfair, but they have felt rage too, only they have to suppress it otherwise the whole place would be in chaos wouldn't it? Darren was a very troubled young man, and we'll never truly know the extent of his problems, but we can remember him for who he was and the way he made our lives better."

I understood exactly what he was saying, I'd spent so much time in that office for my sins but right now I didn't want to leave there. I felt secure and understood for the first time I could remember.

I looked around the office and saw photographs of Mr Law's children on the wall and I realised he was just normal person too, with a family and responsibilities. He wasn't the caustic ogre we made him out to be, yes, he was stern but I suppose it was necessary to keep people like me in line, and to keep a level head in situations like this. He was good at his job. I wanted to tell him that but thought better of it. I'd probably change my mind next term anyway.

I rarely found myself opening up to anybody about anything, I feared if I did then they would see that as my acceptance of a problem, and think I could move forwards. I didn't want to cheat myself knowing I felt different inside so I didn't say anything.

"We're going to be having a memorial service on the day of the funeral as you know," Mr Law said in a shaky voice. "A lot of the children from year nine will be attending; I suppose we could make an exception for a year eight to go if that's really what you want. A lot of people believe funerals are no place for children and I've often been one of those people. However, I think it may provide a little closure for you. I don't want you to look back in years to come and wish you'd attended but were denied the right. I don't want to be the person that stood in your way, so if your parents agree, and I'll type up a letter today, then you're welcome to be there too. I'll arrange transport."
I didn't think my parents would care either way so I nodded my head.

"Yes, I think it might help if I go."

"I can't tell you what to expect," he said, "there will be a great deal of people experiencing the whole grief spectrum, and people won't quite act themselves as you well know." He smiled a little. "I can't tell you what will happen there because I do not know myself but one thing I do know very well, is that most of us will be there looking out for not only you, but all of the people who loved Darren and are representing our school."

"Thank you." Was all I could manage, it seemed insignificant compared to the reassurance I'd just been given, but I hoped he'd understand that I truly meant it from the bottom of my heart.

I dragged myself home after school, my little sister, Beth, who I rarely acknowledged at school because she was considered a 'geek' (I know that sounds every bit as appalling as it was), was going to her friend Lou's house after school, as she lived just around the corner from us. I didn't want to go home on my own that day so I went round her house too. They played upstairs and I sat in the kitchen on my own as nobody was home. I sat in silence with my tears providing my only bitter company.

Then the back door swung open and Bernie came in. Originally he'd moved in as a lodger, as he was studying robotics at the university. He supported himself by working part time and running a martial arts club on Tuesday and Friday at the St. John's Ambulance headquarters. He quickly formed a relationship with Lou's mum, Barbara, and they lived together in this small council house where I was sitting in the kitchen.

Lou hated Bernie, she claimed to never feel comfortable around him, and said once that he played with the zip on her trousers as she sat next to him on the sofa.

Barbara was a mechanic, she had long blonde hair, a dozy expression, and was leader of the St. John's Ambulance meetings I was forced to attend on a weekly basis.

"What's wrong poppet?" Bernie asked me, he looked a little concerned but that may have been because there was a stranger crying in his kitchen.

"Her friend committed suicide last night," said Lou, who was standing in the doorway. "That's why she's upset. They've got to go home now anyway." She stood with her arms crossed, you could sense the animosity in the room.

"Do you want me to give your dad a call?" he asked, as my sister emerged behind Lou.
I immediately said yes. I'm not quite sure why but perhaps it was because I thought my dad wouldn't believe me. Having another adult speak on my behalf would make everything easier. Besides, he wouldn't yell if Bernie were to call him. He respected Bernie and had him upon a pedestal of equal height to himself.

"He said I need to send you home now," said Bernie as he got off the phone.
I'm sure to many children that would have meant going home to open arms; I knew it wouldn't be the case for me though. When you were 'wanted home' in my house, it usually meant there would be trouble. He hadn't even shown any compassion on the phone to Bernie. I wanted to ask him if my dad sounded mad, to gauge what mood he was in but I didn't, it would probably have raised questions and I knew better than to go there.

My dad opened the living room door as we walked into the house. Beth made herself scarce in the back room, probably not wanting to be in the thick of it all.

I wondered what he'd throw at me this time. My friend had died, surely that offered me some kind of morbid immunity.

"Why didn't you come straight home from school?" he asked, with an aloof tone. "It's just, I'm sure if it was that much of a problem for you then the school would have rang us to pick you up."
I sat in silence as usual, not knowing what to say. How was I supposed to know why the school didn't ring? They didn't ring anyone else's parents.

"I just wanted a bit of time to myself I suppose," was all I could offer him as an explanation. I did want to be by myself, it wasn't a lie. It probably wasn't the best answer, I realised as he gave me one of his confused looks.

"But if you wanted to be by yourself, surely you'd have gone for a walk instead? It was your sisters' turn to stay out for a bit after school and you took it upon yourself to go with her, in her time. That's a bit selfish don't you think?"
I shrugged my shoulders as my dry throat tightened again. I wouldn't let that man see me cry. I was glad the school hadn't rang, I couldn't bear to have had to spend the day with him.

"Well?"
My words absconded again, did he want me to admit that I was selfish?
My brain was overloaded, I had this to think about on top of everything else. I wondered what would happen if my brain actually did overload like a computer, would smoke shoot from my ears until I shut down? It was an appealing thought at the time.

70

If I could only shut down for a while, and reboot myself later when my mum got home - she'd understand.

I think he enjoyed watching me squirm, watching as I searched for any answer that might appease him. He leaned back into his chair, I'd seen it enough times to know that it meant he was being less threatening or that he'd be rejecting me soon.

"You know, your sister lost her friend when she was a bit younger than you. She managed to get over it and so will you. Your mum will tell you exactly the same." His voice was soft and I accepted it as the truth.

I wished I hadn't gone home now, I should have gone for that walk instead and avoided him. I'd be in massive trouble but it would have meant less time spent in the living room with him, staring up at that nicotine stained ceiling.

I sat in my room for the rest of the day, I didn't want to eat dinner, though my dad said I was probably on some kind of hunger strike now or attention seeking.

My youngest sister Fiona came upstairs and rifled through the cardboard toy box.

"Are you okay?" she squeaked, with a look of concern on her face. She couldn't have known the circumstances.

"Go away," I shouted at her, "Just go back downstairs."

I knew I'd be in trouble as I heard her run crying to my dad.

Then came the creaking on the stairs under the heavy footsteps of my dad. I'd spent so many years being afraid of him that my ears could tell exactly when he was on his way to tell me off. I often evaluated the heaviness and pace of his footsteps to know whether it would be a physical or emotional punishment.

"Just because you're upset, that's no excuse to talk to your sister like that," shouted my dad, as he flew through the bedroom door. "She's only seven, you're twelve years old. You like bullying kids younger than you do you? Well why don't you just stay up here and be miserable, when you're ready to be part of this family again you can come downstairs."

I hadn't meant to upset my sister, and I should have seen the consequences coming, I just needed to vent a little of my anger and she was the only one there. I wasn't taught how to deal with my emotions properly.
Apologising wouldn't make any difference either, there were no means for redemption in our house. An apology was never acceptable, it always seemed too small an offering according to my dad. Punishment instead would be the slipper, a smack, the belt, or an interrogation by my dad; the amateur psychologist, which would last late into the night. This would normally be followed by days of being shunned by everybody.

Nothing was ever black and white to my dad, everything had a hidden meaning or conspiracy lying in wait.

I lay on my bed and waited for my mum to come home from work, but I must have fallen asleep as I woke up still in my clothes the next morning.

With the same heaviness in my heart as the night before, I crept along the landing and heard my dad snoring from behind his bedroom door. I crept down the stairs, stood in the doorway, and watched my mum as she sat in an armchair drinking a cup of coffee. The clothes horse was in front of the electric fire and she was trying to dry our school clothes. I was going to go back upstairs and leave her in peace but she spotted me and called me through to sit beside her.

I cried as she put her arms around me and told me everything was going to be okay.

"These things happen sometimes, I can't explain why somebody would do something like that, sometimes they're just so unhappy and desperate that they feel there's no other way out." Her words chilled me and I couldn't understand why, perhaps because I knew she was unhappy herself.

"The deputy head said I could go to Darren's funeral if it's okay with you?" I said through sobs.

"I don't know about that. I think you might be too young to experience something like that. Funerals aren't really a place for children."

"But I want to go," I sobbed. "There will be people going from year nine that hardly knew

73

Darren, I don't think it's fair. They're going to sort me out with a lift there and I'll come home straight away afterwards."

I took the crumpled letter out of my pocket, I wanted to keep it safe on my person in case my dad found it and threw it away.

"Okay then." She said softly and signed the form for me.

I don't remember much of the next week and a half, it flew past until the day before Darren's funeral.

I sat in my room almost every evening, often crying myself to sleep. I wanted to write a poem for the school memorial service so I started to use my time constructively. To be honest, as a twelve year old, the poem was never going to win any awards but it held my thoughts and some feelings.

I was sitting on the top bunk bed reading it over to myself when I heard that all too familiar creak on the stairs. This time they were slow, heavy footsteps followed by a loud sigh.

He pushed the bedroom door open slowly.

I showed the poem to my dad and waited for his seal of approval as I thought he should be nearing the last paragraph. I didn't get quite the reaction I'd hoped as he carefully folded it up and put it in his pocket.

"This is too much," he said, with a quiet but stern voice. "You're making too much of it and to be honest, we're all getting sick of you wallowing in your self-pity. It's got to stop. You need to move on and put it behind you, now."

He left the room and I promised myself I wouldn't let him make me cry. Instead, I tore out a fresh sheet of paper and wrote the whole thing down again word for word. It took me a long time to try and draw the border like I had before but this time it looked better. I put it into my school bag, sliding it between one of my text books in case he came back into my room and went through my things as he often did. I'd poured my heart out and he dismissed it.

The funeral was the next day and there was a dress code: if we had a T-shirt of Darren's favourite football team then we were to wear it.
My sister, Beryl, had the exact shirt I needed to fit in with the rest, it was the current seasons strip, she also had the very first version of the shirt which I suppose would only have been described as 'retro' today.
I asked her very politely if I could borrow it for a couple of hours until the funeral was over. She flat out refused.
It was only after I waited up late for my mum to come home, that she would convince Beryl to lend me the older T-shirt. She even held a grudge against me for that and was very reluctant.
The T-shirt had the same badge with the fox's head on as the new one, however, it was missing the white and yellow stripes around the collar and sleeves. I would be standing out like a sore thumb. Kids could be cruel; funeral or not. I should know, I hadn't exactly been pleasant to people at school for

75

their indifferences. If I wasn't wearing the right shirt - they'd notice.

I told Beryl that I'd just go in my school clothes as a last attempt to pull on her heart strings, I told her I'd be teased if I went in the old shirt. She shrugged her shoulders and told my dad that I was being ungrateful.

I got a lecture again and told I was going to be wearing that dull, colour-drained, over-washed old shirt the next day because I was ungrateful.

"If you'd have only asked your sister nicely then she might have let you borrow her other one," said my dad. Beryl looked pleased with herself.

The next morning came and Beryl left for her job as trainee pot washer as a posh hotel in Quorn. I found where she'd hidden the t-shirt and slipped it on underneath the old one. I wasn't going to let anybody in that house ruin Darren's day.

The teachers took their cars and drove us to the crematorium, we'd pretty much have to fend for ourselves once we got there as they were talking to Darren's parents, and I was relieved to be blending in like everyone else.

The funeral was a very unusual experience, and not what I expected at all. As the Hurst pulled up outside the building, people began to cry. There was an arrangement of flowers that spelled out Darren's name, and a coffin that looked a lot smaller than the ones you see on the television. I could feel the tears running down my face and wanted to blame the emotional people around me. I didn't want to cry in front of everyone.

One of the teachers stood me next to a boy called John, he was in Darren's year at school and knew him quite well.

"John will look after you," said the teacher. "He's a nice boy."

We sang hymns, some I didn't know and some I knew from school. We sang, 'Morning Has Broken,' the same song that made me cry that day in school when my mum came in. The teacher was right, John was nice and he didn't mind at all that I cried into his t-shirt as I listened to his voice croak out the words.

As the room was at full capacity, all the children stood at the front and I found myself shielded from Darren's parent's grief.

The red velvet curtains closed in front of Darren's coffin to 'I Will Always Love You' by Whitney Houston, and then it was all over.

We walked quietly out of the crematorium as a line of people stood outside for the next funeral. It seemed so sudden and impersonal, like we were being moved along on a conveyor belt, just like Darren's coffin had been.

We stood outside where the flowers lay, and talked quietly amongst ourselves, I'd found a friend for life in John who didn't leave my side. Some of the children's parents turned up in their shiny cars to take their children home, as my mum was at work and my dad probably still in bed, I went to visit my granddads grave before making my way slowly back to school, despite promising to go straight home. I was consoled by cigarettes and the loudness of the group I was walking with, though inside I felt empty. The teachers had business to attend to before they could come back.

The poem I had written for the memorial, received a lot of praise which became apparent when I got back into school.
I'd asked Mr Elliott to read it out. We hadn't always seen eye to eye in the past but I knew he'd be the right person. He'd told me that lots of tears had been shed amongst staff and pupils, and he believed it may have helped some of them with their grieving process.
Friends told me afterwards that it wasn't so much the words, but the way in which Mr Elliott had read it out. He gave those words meaning and read each one with passion. I'm glad I put my faith in him that day.
I often wished I'd given his parents a copy, but felt it was insignificant at their time of grief.

Chapter Eight.

A short time after Darren's funeral, a lot of things happened. I won the 'Cadet of the Year' award at The St. Johns Ambulance, mainly through pity I think as I didn't exactly try hard there. I remember my mum being cross with me because I wore a pair of trainers with no socks to accompany my uniform, when everybody else was wearing smart black polished shoes. I honestly couldn't have cared less. Things seemed pointless.

I found myself giving up on school and I'd fallen out with Amy too. One of her new friends, Jane, was from a very rough family indeed, and Jane's younger sister had been bullying my little sister, Cara.

Beth and I, had to pick Cara up from an after school club one day, I recall it being Scottish dancing and Jane's sister went there too.
I told Cara to point her out to me told her to stay away from my sister, nothing more - nothing less. It wasn't until we got home that I found the school had rang my mum, they complained that the little girl was so terrified I'd be waiting outside the school for her, she wouldn't go home. Apparently a rumour had circulated that I had a knife which was absolutely preposterous, the only knife I'd ever really held (besides a dinner knife), was my dad's hunting knife that was always locked away. I could hardly believe the accusation when I had it thrown

at me but it didn't surprise me *that* family would make up a story like that.

I got a good telling off from my mum, Dad called me a bully again. I didn't think I was doing anything wrong, I was just sticking up for my little sister, I didn't care who the girls' family thought they were. Shame my family didn't feel the same or have a similar set of morals.

It was a couple of hours later that we had eggs thrown at the living room window. My sisters started screaming hysterically and of course, it was entirely my fault. I offered to clean the windows but my mum said I couldn't be trusted with something so simple. I was a disgrace to the family again. She took me by the ear and marched me down the road, round the corner to the girls' house. She barely spoke a word all the way there but insisted I would be apologising.

When Jane's mum answered the door, my mum pushed me forwards.

"Go on then, apologise for what you did," she shouted, as though she absolutely wasn't my mother.

"Why should I?" I said, "She was picking on Cara."

"I don't deal with these things, Joanne does," she told my mum as she snubbed me.

Joanne was Jane's older sister, she had a reputation for being a bit of a bully but I wasn't bothered at all. My mum on the other hand, I think, felt intimidated by the large lady that stood in the doorway with her flabby, tattooed arms.

"Is that the fat one?" I asked the woman.
She gave me a funny look and her eyes swept back to my mum who looked petrified.

"If she was bullying your daughter, then maybe she deserved having the wind put up her."

"No," said Mum, "It doesn't excuse what Moll did to your daughter. She should know better." I cringed because I'd almost gotten away with it. She wanted the large woman to see she was completely on her side in case it back fired somehow.

"Well there's nothing much I can do now. You said they threw eggs at your windows? Well it's not likely to go any further than that."
My mum thanked her and she shut the door.
I got the silent treatment on the way home but I wasn't bothered. Somewhere underneath her twenty stone frame, that woman had a little respect for me which is more than I had from my own family. I had a little respect for her too; her family stuck together at least.

The next day at school, Amy was sitting opposite me. Her and Jane were laughing at me and making stupid comments.

"I heard you stayed in last night," she laughed. "I hope you had an egg-cellent night?"
I let that comment go and ignored the idiot whilst I got my books ready for the next class. As I turned to leave, she shouted to Jane.

"Oh Jane, stop egg-ing me on, I'm b-egging you."

That's when I lost my temper.

I dropped my books on the floor and strode over to Amy's desk. She looked a little nervous but didn't want to lose face. She had her new friend to back her up which she thought gave her a degree of immunity. Unfortunately for her, I really didn't give a fuck.

"And what egg-xactly do you want?" she asked, as she got to her feet.

I couldn't tell you how quickly she dropped to the floor after I smacked her in her smug face. I was in a tunnel of red and everything was moving slowly. Luckily the teacher wasn't in the room because I'd have almost certainly been suspended and my parent brought into school.

Amy sat on the floor crying and I couldn't have cared less at that moment. Our friendship was over. I didn't need fickle people like her in my life. Perhaps violence wasn't the best way forward, but those types of problems can quickly escalate if you don't put an end to them straight away.

Strangely, Jane started to follow me around that day and wanted to befriend me. I decided it was a safe choice to keep my enemies close, to please my family if anything.

We never did have any more trouble from that family.

I sought solace at the roller disco on a Saturday night. I'd go with my brother, Alex, Beryl and my cousin who I got on really well with. She was the same age as Beryl and her best friend. She was nothing like Beryl though.

We'd spend the whole day getting ready, deciding which outfits we were going to wear. When Beryl was in one of her better moods, she'd lend me some of her clothes but it didn't happen very often.

It was 'the' social event at the time for people our age and we rarely missed a week.

On my twelfth birthday, my parents had bought me a pair of Bauer's, which were popular skates at the time. I remember that day because I was sick and they took me into Leicester on the train to buy them. I'd pestered and pestered them until I wore them down. Besides the sickness, I remember it being am overall good day. Beryl even made me a birthday cake (which I threw up because she put walnuts in it.) There were some good times I remember.

I even managed to find myself a boyfriend there, his friends pestered me until I agreed to go on a date to the cinema with him. He dumped me little less than a week later because he came back to our house that weekend and saw how 'poor' we were.

His dad drove a Mercedes and my dad didn't have a car at the time, was the reason he gave me. He was adamant he wanted to stay friends though. I soon got over him.

I continued to go to the roller disco every week and I learned to be one of the better skaters there.

Because of that, I was popular at school. All the best skaters were. My life was full of ups and downs during this period of my life. Things were always changing.

Perhaps it was because I'd been through a lot in those few months, but I'd developed a strange eating behaviour. It had been my dirty, shameful secret and this is the first time I've ever spoke of it. I used to hoard food.
Packed lunches in particular, regardless of how good they were. I would not sit in the canteen and eat with my friends. I'd go to school with every intention of eating it but when lunchtime came, I'd gotten myself into a pattern of not eating.
At first I threw the sandwiches away, dumping them in the bin at school, then for no particular reason; I started to hold on to them. They gathered at the bottom of my black rucksack for weeks sometimes until they became mouldy.
After my text books began to smell of decomposing food, I decided I had a problem and needed to do something about it.

I remember a school trip to Sherwood Forest one year when I was much younger (before I was such a disgrace to my family), my dad found my long forgotten sandwich box after the summer holidays and the contents were blue and moving. He told me that if I ever did it again, he would force it down my throat.

I was doing the exact same thing all these years later, on a bigger scale, and he knew nothing about it.

It was a terrible memory to be sitting awkwardly in the classroom with my rucksack at my feet, wondering if anybody else could smell its mouldy contents.

I really needed to throw the sandwiches away but I couldn't part with them. That evening I hid them in the walnut wardrobe that was covered with transformers stickers.

I enjoyed a couple of days off from my backpack burden until Beryl complained that the room smelled funny.

I shamefully put the almost liquid sandwiches back into my rucksack which must have provided relief for Beryl's large nose, and nothing was spoken of it again.

The next day I swore I'd get rid of them, I had ample opportunity but told myself I'd do it later. I'd give myself excuses not to and wondered if I could hold on to them for a little longer, but I knew they'd have to go.

The time came at the end of the day when I went into the toilets. It was my last chance to get rid of them. I couldn't use the bin because they'd be found.

My saving grace came in the shape of a sanitary towel bin and that would be where I'd put them and in the weeks to follow. This went on for months as my hoarding continued and went undetected.

I concluded that nobody ever inspected the contents of the bins, why on Earth would they want to?

"It's a power thing apparently," said one of the dinner ladies, "to have control over food, I've read in one of my psychology books that people control what they eat because their lives are so out of control. It could be OCD, it could be hoarding. Whatever it is, it's messed up and this child needs help."

OCD I thought? Not having the faintest idea what she meant. Was it a disease?

My hairs went up on the back of my neck as I walked past her towards the music room.

"I think we know who's been dumping them in there anyway, we'll get to the bottom of it."

I became conscious of my body language and tried not to give anything away, joking with my friends like I was unaffected.

There was never any comeback from that so I thought maybe somebody else got the blame. Perhaps they'd staged the whole thing as to scare me, I don't know. It worked though because I never did it again. I stopped hoarding and found a new compulsion to ease my anxiety instead.

The hoarding would be replaced with secret rituals, This particular compulsion involved tracing the shape of the holy cross on my chest with my finger while muttering 'Please don't let me be in trouble for anything at all. Please, please, please please'.

It may sound completely bizarre to somebody who doesn't understand what compulsions are, however, they're basically something you know to be irrational, yet, you feel the need to follow it through to reduce your anxiety. I suffered from anxiety a lot.

I walked home from school one afternoon and I was in a bad mood about something or another, so I walked on my own. A car pulled up alongside me and asked for directions. I leaned towards the window and tried to point the three teenagers in the right direction. Before my feet had touched the ground, one of them had pulled me into the back seat of the car.

One of the lads looked as if he was being heavily influenced by the two that sat in the front seats. He put his hand over my mouth and dared me to scream, that nobody would hear me anyway. I didn't know what was coming, you hear stories like this all the time but can never appreciate the horror of being in that situation until it happens to you or somebody you care about.

I can honestly say that they were just a trio of stupid teenagers who didn't realise the seriousness of their crime until I was in the car. Apart from one of them putting their hand over my mouth, they didn't lay a finger on me. They drove a little way down the road and let me out.

After I called them a complete bunch of wankers, they drove off laughing and beeping their horn.

I was noticeably distressed when I arrived home and I went to find my dad in the living room. My mum was at work again so he was my only option. I was sure he'd call the police and they might have been able to find the car if we reported it quickly enough.

Through sobs, I explained the whole short ordeal to him, I knew the police would be called but that didn't bother me. Maybe they'd do it to somebody else next time and that person might not get away so easily.

I may have exaggerated with the tears a little, mainly because he listened in a sympathetic manner and I thought I was making a breakthrough with him. I didn't exaggerate the facts though. When I finished recalling the event, he looked at me thoughtfully.

"Did they penetrate you with their fingers?" He asked me.

I stared at him with my jaw agape, wondering what kind of monster he was to ask me something so disgusting.

"No, they didn't do anything to me besides one of them putting their hand over my mouth. I've already told you." I said, refusing any further eye contact.

He leaned forwards to my face and lowered his voice.

"Then don't bother me with your silly fucking problems. You brought it on yourself dressing like a little tart. Why I often think, you know, if you weren't my daughter..."

My head started to ring again and my pulse beat a rhythm out on my eardrums. It was my old friend panic again. I hated it when he used that term 'if you weren't my daughter' It crossed my mind for a moment that my dad was going to kiss me, my stomach felt as though it was beginning to shrivel up. I knew deep down that he'd never do something like that, but he made me feel awkward and uneasy. Like the time he took me shopping with him in town. He'd rarely go out the house on his own, nobody else wanted to go with him and I always found myself with the short straw. I must have been about nine years old at the time and he kept commenting as we walked down the road that people might think I was his girlfriend.

I looked down at my clothes, they were the same as everybody else's. I wore jeans and a t-shirt and hardly looked like a tart at all.

"Oh, and don't go burdening your mum with this either, she's been at work all day, do you understand?"

I nodded my head and took my burden up to my room and it was never mentioned again.

That Saturday the roller disco came around again and we were all excited, we normally played the music we'd taped from the chart show the previous week as we got ready. There was a certain skill required to tape the charts. You had to press pause before the DJ spoke so it wouldn't ruin the song.

My dad had taken up photographing wildlife and informed us that he'd be out that evening. He often went on his own to the dark woods, but preferred it if somebody went with him. There was no way I was going to agree to give up my night at the roller disco, to sit in a dark woodland with him. He desperately wanted my brother to go on his excursions but he wasn't at all interested. He was at the age of vanity.

My dad decided to go to the woods during the day and plan his route through so he'd make less sound at night. I saw how upset he was when Alex flat out refused to go with him so I offered to accompany him. I thought I'd enjoy the roller disco much more if I'd done a good deed and made him happy.

We left about two in the afternoon, roller disco started at half past six, I had four hours to help him find a trail he could use in the woods and get home to get changed.

It was autumn and the darkness came quickly, it was cold and my hair became frizzy in the cold air which I disliked because it was so long. I was worried I'd look like a complete idiot later and people would tease me about it. People went there looking nothing less than immaculate every week - including me.

"You see these twigs and branches?" he pointed to a long walkway through the trees. "I need you to pick them all up and move them to the side."

I stared at the long trail, it would take me days to pick it all up, even if he returned later on that evening, more would have fallen off the trees so it was quite pointless. There's no way I'd be back in time for the roller disco and he knew it.

"If you don't get a move on then you won't be going tonight, it's not difficult to do as I've asked, why do you have to be so goddamn miserable all the time when I ask you to do something?"
I didn't say anything.

"Do you think you're too good to speak to me now?" He asked.
I should have known better than to ignore his previous question, this one was much harder to answer.

"No," I said, "it's just I've been looking forward to it all week."

"Well I know how to get you where it hurts now don't I? If you don't get this trail cleared in the next two hours then you won't be going at all do you understand?"
I started to nod my head but thought better of it.

"Yes." I said quietly.

"That's more like it."
I carried on moving the twigs and branches solidly for the next two hours, my hands were cut and bleeding. My hands and fingernails were covered in mud and grass stains. I felt dirty and I wouldn't have time for a bath when I got in.

We got home moments before Beryl and Alex were about to leave. I got the third degree from her as I ran upstairs to get ready.

"We were going to go without you," she said. "You should put some deodorant on at least."
I ran into the bathroom and washed my hands, I was too young for makeup at that age so that saved me

91

two hours of getting ready. I threw on my clothes, I didn't have music to listen to, instead I listened to her constant whining from downstairs, that if I wasn't ready in ten seconds then they were going to leave without me.

My dad was in a bad mood with me because of the 'attitude' I'd shown him in the woods. There were many days like this throughout my childhood where I just couldn't win. The sacrifices I made to live a half normal life were incredible.

An hour passed after we'd returned home that night, and a police riot van pulled up outside our house.

We watched from the window as they unloaded my dad out the back and walked him to the front door. We listened as they explained everything to my mum, how my dad had been found on the university campus hiding in some bushes with his binoculars. Somebody had seen him and reported him to the police. He insisted he was looking for exotic animals but I don't think the police were very convinced.

Chapter Nine.

Dad decided it was about time he got himself mobile so he applied for his provisional license. It gave him the ability to ride a motorcycle up to a 125cc engine with an L plate.
He bought himself a Honda CM125 in black and chrome. It was his pride and joy for a long time, though he dreamed of an Electra Glide or a Goldwing.

I remember how he used to trawl the Ad-Mag every week. He'd look for motorbike leathers and once he'd bought a set for himself, he used to buy them to 'do up' with black shoe polish to make them look as good as new to sell them on for a profit.
Because I was the only one who went on his trips to the woods with him, it was me that got to go out in the evenings with him on his motorbike. To begin with it was a lot of fun until the novelty wore off. After that, I didn't enjoy the late nights and having to get up for school the next morning.
At least we didn't have to walk to the woods anymore now we had transport.

It wasn't all bad memories though, we'd sometimes go and sit by the dead tree and he'd take his CB radio with him, throw the antennae up and over a tree to speak to my mum. He'd tell her to put the kettle on and make us some poached egg sandwiches because we were on our way home.

There were the odd few good memories that I owe to my dad, while most of my friends were playing with their dolls, I was learning to shoot his Ripley rifles and crossbows in the back garden, watching him as he made all his own steel moving targets for us to shoot down.

Other times on our outings, he'd leave me alone in the dark woods. These weren't such good memoiries. He'd assure me that it was to improve my night vision and sensory skills. I could barely see anything as it was because of my poor eyesight.

One evening we rode into Leicester city centre because the council had hung up the Diwali lights. It was an amazing experience to be surrounded by so many different twinkling lights travelling at a high speed down the main road.

At around midnight, we stopped in a small village called Quorn and Dad decided that he wanted to drive up to Swithland Reservoir.

We turned down Wood Lane and rode into the pitch black as we left the street lights behind. It was so dark there that I was concerned he wouldn't see the sharp bends in time and we'd get thrown off. I envisioned it happening and I must have held my breath for most of the way.

When we reached the Reservoir, we got off and looked at the mist floating eerily across the water. It reminded me of that song by Deep Purple 'Smoke on the Water.' Our next door neighbour would wake the whole neighbourhood up with it every weekend as he played it on his electric guitar in his back garden.

"Me and Derrick came up here in his car one night," he told me. "We got such a shock when we drove round the corner and saw a body hanging in the trees. We called the police but something like that, you know, kind of scares you doesn't it? People do it all the time around here. There's also a headless monk that walks around. Anyway, when we drove past the hanging man, something hit the side of Derrick's car continuously 'BANG BANG BANG' until we reached the end of the road. We didn't dare stop to see what it was, but when we got back, the car was covered in dents all over. Spooky eh?"

Then he asked me to stand where I was and not move while he rode off on his motorbike. He wanted me to tell him how bright his lights looked from a distance, and to judge how far away he was before he came into view.

Then he rode off until I could no longer see or hear him.

I wasn't really afraid of the dark, I never had been one of those children, but at that moment I was petrified. I was twelve years old, stood in the pitch black - alone.

There was a hotel down the road that we passed on the way in and I was sure that if I could get there, someone would be willing to help me get home.

I was frozen with fear as thoughts of the hanging man pushed itself to the forefront of my mind. I was scared that if I moved even an inch, I would see him staring at me from the treetops of the wood on the other side of the stone wall. The fear was so real that I could almost feel him behind me, blowing the cold air onto my neck.

I concentrated hard on the darkness at the end of the road and willed my dad to come back soon. Then I began to think of Darren and the cause of his death, my good friend that I had only fond memories of, soon became the object of my terror.

I thought to myself: *'What if I turn around and see Darren hanging in the tree? What if he smiles and waves at me? Will his eyes be open and glazed over like a fish on a cold slab?'* The disgusting thoughts make me sick with tears and I hated myself for allowing his memory to be tainted like that.

I blamed my dad, the man who was nowhere to be seen. I wouldn't have put it past him to leave me there for a lot longer, and I thought about finding that hotel. If such a thing as the hanging man did exist, if Darren wanted to creep up and scare the shit out of me, then it would happen regardless. I had nothing to lose. *'The dead can't hurt me'*, I told myself over and over again through my tears, *'only the living, only my dad.'*

It was such a large open space, but in the darkness, I could hear my own footsteps as they crunched the gravel, and my own shallow breath. I decided that as long as I looked confident, anything that might have been watching me would leave me alone. Then out of the blackness came my dad on his stupid motorbike. I had so much adrenaline pumping through my body that I swear I could have kicked him off as he rode past.

"Yes your lights are very bright," I snapped, as I jumped on the back.

"Why are you being so mardy?" he asked me, oblivious to the act of cruelty he'd subjected me to.

"Because it's cold."

"Because you're a scaredy-cat more like," he laughed. You need to toughen up a bit."

And toughen up I did, because he didn't just ride off and leave me at the reservoir, he'd take me to the cemetery and leave me there too. He'd always park up in the area where Darren's headstone was, and ride off for what seemed like a lifetime. As my fear lessened, my hatred for him grew stronger.

Chapter Ten.

I have some very fond memories of school trips I've been on. When I was at primary school, my parent saved up so I could go to the Lake District. There was only room for ten children to go so it was on a first come - first served basis. I'll always be grateful to my parents for paying for me to have the experiences and adventures I had.

The caretaker that cleaned up my accident on my first day of school, would be the responsible adult organizing it all with a couple of other teachers.

I remember how we squeezed into a very small, very stuffy minibus, and after a few long hours, we were there.

We stayed in a youth hostel that had some beautiful surrounding gardens with small waterfalls. We were allowed to roam freely on our own outside, and I often wondered if my parents would have let me go if they'd have known the extent of freedom we had.

We climbed a mountain called Scafell Pike which had a height of 978 meters, and a mountain called Helvellyn which stood at 950 meters. We also tried abseiling which I really enjoyed.

I was faced with a dilemma when I was there, either spend twenty pence on a phone-call home or spend it on Kendal mint cake. Needless to say, I suffered a sickening guilt after eating all that Kendal mint cake.

In the evenings, the staff would take us to a local pub and shower us with cola and crisps. They gave us money for the jukebox and we spent it all on the tracks from Dirty Dancing. We all danced around in the pub until well into the night as the staff drank their funny coloured drinks and laughed amongst each other. It would be a holiday I'd never forget.

As I was now in year eight, the school had a trip to Wales planned. We'd be going for a week. Both Alex and Beryl had been on the trip when they attended the same school years before. Our parents were called because Alex had managed to get his leg caught under a roundabout at a park. I felt terribly sorry for him when he arrived home shortly afterwards with an old man's walking stick that he had to use for a couple of weeks.

My parents found the money to send me on the trip, I was looking forward to spending a week away from the house. At twelve, it was a big deal to be parent free, especially as I had so little freedom at home. When the day finally arrived, I was relieved they would no longer be able to use it as a punishment, threatening me that I wouldn't be able to go if I didn't own up to things I hadn't done - things my siblings blamed on me during 'gripe night'.

In Wales, we stayed at a mountain centre surrounded by forest. It was exclusive to us that week as I suppose the safety aspects of taking children away had been reassessed by then to a degree.

Again I enjoyed abseiling, and climbed a mountain called Cnicht. We were supposed to be climbing Snowdon but the weather was unpredictable.

We canoed on a huge lake and I remember the overwhelming sense of freedom being on my own in that wide open space. I was one of a few that didn't capsize that day. We also went gorge walking and ended the day by jumping into a waterfall. The feeling of the water pushing me down to the bottom of the lake was fantastic. Some of us were a little nervous to begin with but our teachers assured us that it was an opportunity of a lifetime, and we'd regret it if we didn't take it. It was a marvellous memory.

One of the evenings, we went to Tremadog Bay and played in the sand dunes in the dark. It was almost like being on another planet as the sand glowed whitely and the sky glowed an eerie blue.

We played a form of manhunt in the forest that surrounded our accommodation, it was dark and the teachers used a hut which was to be our headquarters. I can't remember the actual nature of the game, but I recall we had to hunt for things other than people. My friend lost her shoe in the mud, I remember that much as she hopped back to HQ. I felt free as I ran about that forest in the dark whilst most of the other children stuck together because they were scared. This gave me the upper hand in the game.

Back in the dormitory, I had one of the top bunk beds that were stacked three beds high. I shared the dorm with eight other girls, and there was a smaller one for some of the others who didn't quite fit in.

I don't know where the cigarettes came from but one of the girls passed them around, we hung out of the window whilst we took it in turns to fan the smoke alarm with our towels.

One of the girls, Sarah, said that she was going to tell the teacher about our smoking. I couldn't afford to have them call my parents, and I'm ashamed to say that we thought the best way to silence her was through intimidation.

One of the girls told Sarah that she'd slap her if she grassed us up. I made a shadow puppet on the ceiling in the shape of a dog, I was quite good at shadow puppets.

I called the dog 'Sarah' and mimicked her voice, joking that she was going to tell the teachers about our smoking.

She cried and darted across the room to the door and left to tell on us.

A few minutes later, one of the teachers came in and shouted at us all. We were told to bring our suitcases through to the living area, and the teachers searched our items for cigarettes. They didn't find any as we'd thrown them out the window.

"I'm surprised at you especially," said the teacher, as she looked at me.

I was especially surprised that she said that and I shrugged it off.

Sarah and a couple of the other girls moved into the smaller dormitory which left the 'bad ones' in mine.

I felt a little bad the next morning when Sarah came down to breakfast, her eyes were red and puffy. She was still snivelling as the teachers gathered around her. I complained that she was just attention seeking. She started to become hysterical and then she was sick into her breakfast bowl. I caught a glimpse of one of the teachers rolling their eyes as they tried to calm her down. I was pretty sure Sarah lived a life completely opposite to mine. She received attention every time she clicked her fingers or turned on the tears.

On the coach on the way home, I listened to Whigfield, 'Think of You' and Jam & Spoon, 'Right in the Night' on my Walkman, though it wasn't exactly a Walkman, but a much cheaper brand.
My dad was waiting on his motorbike as the coach pulled up outside the school. He loaded my oversized suitcase onto the back of his bike and secured it with a bungee rope. He rode home slowly shouting at me to keep up with him.
It was back to reality for me.

Chapter Eleven.

Around the time I turned thirteen, I began training at Bernie's martial arts club regularly. My parents said I was spending far too much time alone in my room and that I was becoming a hermit. I thought my dad was a hypocrite as he rarely went out of the house on his own.

I didn't want to go to the classes, I'd already been forced into St. John's Ambulance which I hated - now this.

All I wanted to do was sit in my room and play my keyboard. My parents had bought me a keyboard for Christmas, and I was becoming quite good. I remember seeing the large wrapped present on the floor that morning.

"I wonder what that is?" I asked my dad at the time, and he told me that it was probably a coffin.

I went to my first class with Beth and Lou, it went okay, I don't know exactly what I was expecting. At least it kept me out the house and out of blames way.

I struggled to take Bernie seriously, I imagined people who taught these classes were big and covered with rippling muscles, Bernie was around eight stone, looked like a hippy, and bounced when he walked.

There was a whole mixture of people that trained there: soldiers, policemen, and even a stunt-man. They all had an unspoken respect for him and hung on his every word.

Barbara used to train there too, though she always looked worn down and I suspected her heart wasn't really in it.

Bernie was very welcoming and didn't make me do anything I wasn't comfortable with, although he had a seemingly magical way to get me to participate in things I was unsure of.

The classes were on every Tuesday and Friday, and I'd soon get my own blue uniform with sewn on logo.

I became more interested when I witnessed what Bernie was capable of. He could throw men almost twice his own weight halfway across the room. He'd have them in positions they couldn't wriggle out of and some; almost in tears.

At the club, I studied a plethora of different styles; Judo, Wing Chun, Ju-Jitsu, Muay Thai, Wushu, Lau Gar and Kick Boxing. At the end of each session, we'd have the opportunity to practice sparring with each other.

Bernie was always really nice to me, I wouldn't say he singled me out so much at that particular time, though I did notice that he did seem to be staring at me an awful lot, and he was always there behind me when I'd turn around. I thought it was just my imagination.

I soon flew up the grading system and was a green belt before I knew it. I'd overtaken my little sister Beth, and Lou also.

It was compulsory to learn the Cantonese and Mandarin terms for every sequence of movements we learned. Because I was obsessed with training, I also became obsessed with the language and dialects. My head could always be found in a book of something that was relevant.

If you were unable to do certain things from the grading syllabus, you wouldn't move up the grade. Bernie was very strict.

He'd created his own style of kung fu that was a mixture of everything, he developed his own kata (a sequence of movements [also referred to as form]), and he gave them the most peculiar names like: Roland Trip (for green belt), The Scales (for yellow belt.) As his students, we often thought they had some philosophical meaning behind them because we looked up to him in such a manner. However, this wasn't the case and they held an entirely different (drug related) meaning.

We'd become almost like a small family at the club.

My parents were pleased that I was finally getting out of the house from under their feet, and I developed a quiet confidence which meant I was a little quieter and slightly less obnoxious. They continually showered Bernie with praise because he made me a 'better person,' and he'd made the family better in some way, too.

He'd sit and listen to my dad talk about his conspiracy theories, even if he did think it was absolute nonsense.

When I wasn't training at the club, I was training at home. It took over my life. I asked my parents to install the punch bag they bought me for my birthday in the back room. I practiced stretching to increase my flexibility which made no end of difference to my performance. My legs became stronger, as did every other muscle in my body. It became my outlet, a way for me to release all the pent up anger inside of me.

Bernie always seemed to be making a huge effort with Lou, and she always seemingly threw it back in his face. I was jealous of the attention he showed her because she appeared so ungrateful. Part of me really wanted him as my own father, we could train every day. I hated that Lou wasted this opportunity.

Bernie held a bonfire night in November, and invited all of the students from the class.
He gave me a couple of bottles of French beer whilst we were alone in the kitchen. It was a grimy kitchen with a brown beaded curtain that hung over the door.

"You look ravishing tonight," he said. "In fact, I could ravish you myself."
I didn't quite understand what he meant, but I took it as a compliment anyway.
I was a little merry that evening and remember almost falling into the bonfire. For the first time in a while, I had begun to enjoy my life.

On Valentine's Day the following year, I was surprised to receive a card through the post. The handwriting looked exactly like my dad's, though Bernie had similar handwriting too. They both put that strange line and the end of their 's'.
I was too young to understand the meaning of the card but as an adult, it chills me.
It read: 'Dear Valentine, when I think of you, my heart starts to throb (not to mention certain other parts.)' My parents thought it was funny and not at all inappropriate.

My dad began to use training as a form of punishment for me. Time after time, I'd be blamed for crimes I hadn't committed, if I didn't own up to them, I'd be banned for that week. He said he knew how to 'get me where it hurts'.
Then my brother, Alex, started training sometime afterwards and brought his friends along with him. There wasn't enough room in Bernie's car for us all so he stopped picking me up and we caught the bus down instead.
I was concerned Bernie would lose interest in me from then on, so I began to train harder than ever. Alex really looked up to Bernie, but it wouldn't be long before he came of the age where he wanted to go out with his friends and he stopped training. That was when Bernie picked me up and dropped me off again.

On the drive home from class one evening. I told Bernie how I played the keyboard and had been bought one for Christmas. It was a music lesson at school that inspired me to start playing. We had to compose a piece of music to reflect a poem we had been reading. My music teacher was so impressed with what me and my friend Lindsey had created, that he had us perform it in front of the whole school.

John started to hang around me a lot more at school, and I told him about the classes. It wasn't long before he brought along his younger brother, and they became regulars too.
Bernie seemed to snub me for a while afterwards, and I could only assume it was because I'd brought a boy to join up. He'd make the classes difficult for John, and when he'd drop me off after class, he'd tell me that John was holding me back and how I'd never reach my full potential with people like him around me.
John's mum took some Tai-Chi classes from Bernie's friend, Brian. He always mocked Brian and said he was a useless instructor and a hypochondriac. I'd met Brian a few times and though he was a lovely man.

Bernie would ask for my assistance to demonstrate moves in the class, and on many occasions he'd apologise because his hands ended up in inappropriate places. He'd also ask me to help him put the equipment away after class in the cupboard in the small room upstairs. I'd often find myself in there alone with him, and he'd play with my hair as I stacked the mats into a pile, or he'd rub his hand up and down my back.

"You know I've been thinking," he said to me one day as he drove me home, "I play the guitar, I don't know an awful lot about music but I'm sure with my knowledge, I could help you to learn the keyboard better. I used to be in a band during the eighties, and we supported a well known band at the time."

"That would be brilliant," I said, thinking he was warming to me again. Thank you so much."

"You're welcome, you need to ask your parents first though if it's okay. I wouldn't tell them that I offered to teach you though, they already think they put on me enough. I wouldn't want them to think I was trying to replace them as parents," he joked.

Monday nights had become the evening of family entertainment, my dad called it our 'Gripe Night', and it was a chance for people to air their concerns over the other family members' behaviour. Unfortunately, I would usually be everybody's target, and I'd be the one left sitting in the middle of the room on the interrogation chair until the early hours, whilst my dad tried to get inside my head and break me.

It was midweek when I asked them if they'd mind Bernie teaching me to play the keyboard.

"Is there anything that man can't do?" said my dad, full of admiration for him. My parents agreed that Bernie could teach me at our house on Wednesday evenings.

The first couple of lessons were very formal, we sat in the kitchen with my new keyboard as he tried to make sense of the music theory information he'd printed out.

"John's a nice boy isn't he? I suppose you spend a lot of time together at school don't you?" he asked as he studied my face.

"Yeah he's okay," I said. "It's not as though he's my boyfriend or anything though. We just hang out."

"I just don't want him to hold you back, that's all Petal," he smiled.

"He doesn't," I assured him.

Bernie obviously knew nothing about music theory, but I appreciated the effort he put in to learn all about it to teach me. Unaware it was one of his grooming techniques to provide himself with unsupervised access to me.

One Wednesday evening, Bernie had to cycle over because Barbara needed his car. He brought an old brown satchel with him.

The keyboard lesson would start later than normal that evening because my dad wanted to run another of his theories past him.

When we sat in the kitchen uninterrupted, he pulled out a bunch of half a dozen red roses and gave them to me.

I was quite shocked, I'd never been bought flowers before. I had no idea why he had bought them for me. He looked a little awkward when he saw my confused expression, but he quickly justified his actions.

"Because you're doing so well with your keyboard lessons, I bought these for you. You might want to tell your parents that you got them from somebody at school," he said. "It's just that if they see I've bought you flowers, they'll think I'm trying to take their place as a parent, which I'm not of course."
I waited until the coast was clear and I ran upstairs to my room to put them in my school bag.

The gifts didn't stop there either, Bernie bought me a pair of boxing gloves and other training equipment I mentioned I was saving up for. He'd always wait until after class was over to give them to me, before reminding me that it was our secret. I was to tell people I'd won them during a sparring competition at the club. Afterwards he'd always ask me for a hug and say that it was okay to hug him because he wasn't a pervert like my dad.
When no questions were asked, he began to hold competitions at the club, knowing that I'd likely win the majority of them. The prizes were always a day out to a seminar, or a day out to a tournament with him. My parents would just let me go along with him. It was only ever me and Bernie that went.

The next time I 'won' a day out with Bernie, he would be taking me to a tournament in London. He'd been showering me with little gifts all day and

111

he finally had me on my own outside the hall near some vending machines.

"I need to tell you something, and I don't want you to get upset," he said, as he became serious. I wondered what I'd done wrong, my stomach started to flip.

"It's just that after today, well I don't think I'm going to be able to teach you anymore, the piano lessons are going to have to stop too." He looked for a reaction.

"But why?" I said, "What have I done?" I felt as though my heart had just been stomped on. I'd been having a really good day, why did he have to ruin it by saying this?

"It's nothing you've done really, not that you know about anyway." he said.

"What have I done?" I begged, "Whatever I've done, I'm sorry. Please don't stop me training, it's the only thing I have."

"I've fallen for you Petal, that's what this is about."

"Oh." Was all I could offer him. Suddenly all the gifts made sense.

I suppose after the initial shock of it, I suppose I was quite flattered in an awkward kind of way. I couldn't bear to give up my training and would do whatever it took to hang on to it. Training was my life, along with the piano lessons. It was what I felt defined me as a person.

"Although there is another option," he said, in a hushed tone. "It could be our little secret, nobody

would need to know a thing. I suppose it depends how you feel about that."
I shrugged. I'd had a boyfriend before, nothing serious at my age. I didn't know exactly what Bernie would have been expecting from me, but I could always call it off if I needed to."
He held my hand and smiled.

"If you stick around long enough, I might even make you an instructor and you can run your own classes. Would you like that?"

"Yes I would, that's what I've always wanted to do." I said, almost completely forgetting the conversation we'd just had.

"Better keep it quiet then, just act normally around your parents and don't tell a soul that I plan to make you an instructor. It would upset a lot of people at the club because they've been training a lot longer than you and they'll never be good enough. You don't want to make people jealous do you Petal?"

"No," I said. "It's our little secret."
On the drive home, we pulled into a little country lane on the outside of town. He told me to get into the back seat of the car and he did the same. I froze on the seat as he climbed in and straddled me, touching my face and hair. He rubbed his body up against mine and I sat perfectly still.
This is what it's like to have an adult relationship then, I thought to myself.
Bernie got back into the driver's seat, and I stayed in the back, not speaking a word as he dropped me off at my house.

He turned around to face me as he pulled onto the driveway.

"Remember Petal, it's our secret. I'll see you at training on Tuesday."

I smiled at him and got out of the car feeling very confused. I could still go to the club and have my piano lessons so I'd just go along with it. I'd even be getting my own club eventually, Bernie had promised.

I didn't let the relationship aspect plague my thoughts too much, I was looking to the future, something I'd never been able to do before.

Chapter Twelve.

I won't lie, I used to smoke at school whenever I could get my hands on cigarettes. Because my dad had quit, I had to rely on others to provide them and as I looked quite old for my age, the kids used to send me into the shop at lunchtime to buy them. In exchange I'd take fifty percent of the packet.

English was my favourite lesson, I loved to read poetry and hear other people reading it too. I took separate lessons for language and literature, taught by Mr Coates, my favourite teacher, a very handsome teacher at that. He was in his mid-twenties and when he read Shakespeare, he sent my heart fluttering away. My English had improved because I tried so hard to be good at it.
For a short while I had a crush on him, one that would be short lived, one that would come to an abrupt, jealous end quite quickly.

He came into the classroom one day sporting a wedding ring and my classmates asked him about it. He told us that he'd got married and would soon be off on his honeymoon.
I felt angry and cheated even though that lovely man never gave any indication whatsoever that he was interested in me. I'm sure he'd have been mortified had he known the truth.
Because I felt my silly rejection so sorely, I decided that I was no longer going to be his top student.

Instead I would become disruptive, impossible to teach, rude, and make his life miserable.

He used to wear the oddest socks you could imagine, they were a strange mustard colour and we always teased him about it. I decided to go a step further and bought a few pairs from the market one Saturday.

I suppose a lot of the bullying that went on in that classroom was premeditated. My friends and I, moved from the back of the classroom to the front and we each put on a pair of the mustard coloured socks I'd bought. We rolled up our jeans and poked out legs out under the desk so he could clearly see them. We also used to shout "Sweat rings!" when he'd take off his blazer, and continually talk about it until he put it back on.

Eventually we broke his spirit and he'd get angry and storm out the classroom. Looking back, I'm ashamed of my behaviour. He had a wonderful gift to teach and we threw it back in his face.

It seemed every negative thing I said or did had a profound effect on people, I didn't realise at the time that it was because I executed everything with a concoction of hate and pure desperation. I had an overwhelming urge to destroy everything that was good.

I walked through the door after school and my dad shouted me into the living room.

"I want to speak with you," he said. "Sit down."

"I'm just going to take my bag upstairs."

"No you're not. Sit down."

116

I sat quietly on the sofa, wondering what it would be this time. I wondered if I was smart enough to wriggle my way out of it.

"You've been smoking, I can smell it on you." I knew how to get out of this one.

"I haven't," I lied. "My friends smoke and the smell must have gone on me because I stood near them."

"You're lying, I don't believe for one second that you'd just stand around and not join in. I know exactly how your mind works. You're so desperate to be accepted. I wouldn't put anything past you. Drink, drugs, the list goes on."

I'd never touched drugs in my life. There was no use arguing with him, once his mind was made up there was only one right answer – his.

"I'm going to give you a choice," he said, with a smug expression. "If you're not smoking, then let me look in your school bag. If you're not guilty then you have nothing to hide. Or you can choose not to let me look, I'll know that you have cigarettes in there and you'll be banned from training for two weeks. The choice is yours."

He looked quite pleased with himself as he settled back into his armchair.

"I don't want you to look in my school bag," I said, my eyes fixed on the floor.

"I knew it," he said triumphantly, "I fucking knew you were smoking. You're grounded for two weeks, no training, no piano lessons and if I find out you've been smoking again, I'll make you eat a whole pack of the damn things."

"I suppose I deserve it." I said quietly.

I could live without training for two weeks, what I couldn't live with, was my dad discovering what was really in my school bag. There were no cigarettes, only my exercise books with drawings of my dad with male genitalia on his head. Scribed underneath were captions like; 'my dad is a wanker' and other colourful language. I thought the discovery of this would be much harder to explain so I took the punishment instead.

I rarely lied because as my dad used to say *'you can lock a thief out but there's nothing you can do with a liar'*.

At first I accepted the punishment, but I soon became resentful and wanted to go training again. I tried all manner of things to get my freedom back and redeem myself. I did extra chores and I went on those miserable walks with my dad but it changed nothing. He wanted to get me where it hurt.

It was Friday morning and later, I was supposed to be at training.

I knew Bernie would wonder where I was and he'd probably be angry if he came to pick me up to discover I was grounded. So that morning when I got on the bus to take me to school, I decided not to go.

As the bus pulled up to the main stop when most of the children got on, I pushed past them and jumped off.

"Where are you going?" Lindsey asked, "Are you bunking off?"

118

"So what if I am?" I shrugged.

"Can I come with you?"

"No you can't."

"Well, where you going?"

"Well, I'm not going to school that's for sure. I don't know where I'm going, here and there."
My friends looked at each other, almost willing somebody else to jump off with me.

"You'll get grassed up you know, all the geeks are watching."

"I probably will but they'll just have to deal with things when I come back pissed off won't they?" I raised my voice so they could hear, "I'm going to enjoy my day off, see you keen beans later."

"Enjoy your day off Ferris Bueller." Lindsey laughed.
I watched the bus pull off and I headed towards Bernie's house. I knew Barbara would be at work and Bernie didn't work Friday's. Underneath my brazen exterior I was a bundle of nerves. I had to tell Bernie the reason I wouldn't be at class that evening, I was sure he'd be pleased to see me. I was worried that if I didn't tell him in person, he'd think it was something he'd done wrong.

In spite of my terrible eyesight, I was able to make out the bonnet of his blue sierra poking out from behind the bushes as I drew closer. I didn't know what I was going to say when he opened the door. I'd skived off school so I could quickly give him what I thought was an important message. I

119

believed he was the only real friend I had, and I needed his help to escape from my family.

He looked almost horrified as he opened the door.

"Aren't you supposed to be at school?" he asked. "Does anybody know you're here?"

"Nobody knows where I am, except me, and you now."

"You'd better come in before somebody see's you on the doorstep, because then we'll both be in trouble."

Bernie made me a drink of coffee that tasted suspiciously like alcohol. He said it was an Irish coffee and it could calm my nerves. I drank it regardless of the fact that it burned my throat on the way down.

"So why have you bunked off? You know your parents will go mental when they find out don't you?"

"They've grounded me because my dad thought I had cigarettes in my school bag." I went on to explain the whole story and he laughed.

"I hate to be the one to tell you this, but your dad's mentally ill." He scoffed.

"There's a counsellor at school that I talk to quite a lot." I said.

"Counsellor?" Bernie interrupted.What have you been saying to him? You haven't mentioned me have you? For god sake Moll, if you mention me then that will be the end of everything," there was an unmistakable panic to his voice.

"I haven't mentioned you at all," I lied, "only my dad and the way things are at home."

I had told the counsellor about Bernie but only to say how much he'd been helping me. I liked talking about Bernie to people. The school counsellor had only ever replied that he thought it was good I had a positive influence in my life.
He relaxed his tone a little and suddenly seemed less uptight.

"It's just that if people find out then they'll split us up. You'll be put into care and I won't be able to teach you anymore which would be a shame because I plan to make you an instructor soon so you can run your own classes."
My face must have lit up, he knew I always wanted to teach my own class.

"If I can't teach you anymore, there would be no point in me sticking around here. I'll probably end up moving away and that would be the end of that."

"I don't want that to happen." I said.

"You just need to be a little careful who you speak to then Petal, there are a lot of narrow minded, spiteful people out there who can't bear to see other people happy. People like your parents, people like your counsellor at school.

Bernie's phone rang a while later and we instantly recognised the number - it was my dad.

"No Jim, I've not seen her today," said Bernie. "What time did she go missing?"
He paused while my dad spoke, though I couldn't hear what was being said.

"Give me ten minutes, Jim, and I'll help you come and look for her, okay?"

He paused again.

"It's no problem, see you soon."

He hung up the phone and turned to me with a serious expression.

"I don't know what you're going to do but your dad sounds furious. They're out looking for you." He climbed out of bed naked and walked towards the wardrobe to get himself some clothes out. We hadn't done 'everything' but there wasn't much he hadn't asked me to do.

He sat down on the edge of the bed and pulled back his long greying ponytail using his red Afro comb.

"So what are you going to do? You know you need to go home at some point don't you?"

"I will go home, but I don't know what I'm going to say when they ask me where I've been."

"I don't know what to suggest Petal, I'm not condoning lying, but maybe you could tell them you skipped school because of bullying? You'll have to find somewhere to hide out for a bit while I go over to your house."

I shrugged.

"If you tell me where you're going to be, I can try and keep them away from the area you see, and I'll convince your dad to take it easy on you when you go home."

"Can I stay here for a bit?" I asked. "They won't find me here will they? Barbara won't be back for hours yet and I'll make sure I'm gone before she does."

I was desperate, the weather was terrible outside. The wind had picked up and the rain was thrashing the windows. I couldn't have picked a better day to skive off.

"Absolutely not, I'm sorry Petal but just supposing she comes home sick or something, what will she say if she see's you here? I can't stress how important it is that nobody finds out about us because they just won't understand."

"I'll go and sit in the park around the corner for a couple of hours then I suppose." I said.

"Come on Moll, don't be like that. It'll be over soon, you might have to put up with your dad raving at you for a while but just remember what a moron he is and you'll be okay."

I followed him downstairs and he opened the front door to let me out. He walked carefully down to the bottom of the drive first to make sure nobody was about.

"Bloody hell it's freezing out there." He said.

"Can I borrow a coat please?" I asked, looking out at the heavy rain.

"I can't Petal, sorry. If you turn up at home wearing my coat, they're going to know I've seen you and they'll start asking you all kinds of questions. You know what your dad's like, I'm sure you don't want that do you?"

"No I suppose not."

I stepped out into the cold reality of consequences and made my way around to the park. It looked nothing like I remembered when I got there. The old Portakabin had been pulled down and all that stood were a couple of the old climbing frames and a set of swings.

I sat on one of the swings and looked out at the space where the Portakabin used to be. There was a rectangle of concrete which I presumed had been its foundations. I'd had more fun and good memories in the space of that rectangle than I'd had in my whole life.

I moved from the swings that were always my favourite when I was younger, and I took shelter from the rain underneath the smaller of the two climbing frames. I examined the wood and smiled as I saw some familiar carvings;

'Moll woz 'ere 1991', and 'Beryl loves Mark IDST' (If Destroyed Still True).

I cried for my wasted youth and I mourned for the family I'd never have. Suddenly it didn't feel so great to be me. If I was so great, why did I hurt people? And why was I hiding underneath a fucking climbing frame alone, on a school day? I was beginning to wish I'd just gone to school.

Everything around me was functioning fine - I was dysfunction.

I climbed out and stared at the slide for a moment, I remembered playing in that exact spot as a child, in this kind of weather too. We'd collect snails and race them down the slide.

I limped my heavy heart to the next climbing frame. I remember it looked huge when I was younger and was unable to use the monkey bars. This was the 'big kids' climbing frame, most of them walked along the top of the bars but I could never do that for fear of slipping through the gaps.

I climbed to the top and sat on the end bar, my feet dangling about six feet from the ground, watching the lightening as it lit up the cornfield which sat behind the park.

I closed my eyes as the rain pelted my face, and offered myself to the blue electric that shot across the sky. I willed it to hit me just the once and finish me off.

It didn't happen so I jumped down to the ground and decided it was time to stop feeling sorry for myself. I wanted to go for a little walk, somewhere I hadn't dared go for a long time.

The conifer trees still stood tall at the park entrance, when we were younger, we used to climb onto the concrete post where the old gate used to be and we'd pull the conifer down as far as possible. One of us would hold on tight and the others would let it go. We'd shoot high up into the air until the old man who lived next to them came out with his rifle and started firing pellets at us.

I walked around the corner until I came to the golf course where Darren had taken his life a couple of years earlier. I stood at the entrance and hesitated, until I remembered that people were out looking for me.

My dad had been trying to get me up there ever since Darren died, he liked to take the dog for a walk and to look for golf balls in the dark with his image intensifier. I could never bring myself to go with him. I just wasn't ready.

It looked just like an ordinary golf course and suddenly the whole thing felt impersonal. I wondered where the spot would have been, the place Darren would have spent his last few moments on Earth. An overbearing tree caught my attention, underneath lay a withered rose and I knew I'd found Darren's tree.

I walked over to it and a feeling of utter helplessness hit me like a brick wall. My legs went weak and I struggled to stand up. I tried to control my breathing and control my tears as I wanted to scream out. I didn't want to lean on the tree to steady me, it had already taken my friend and I felt as though I didn't have much fight left in me.

I wondered what had been on Darren's mind when he climbed that tree, when he inched closer to the branch he'd use. The pain and despair he must have felt, perhaps he felt nothing at all. Maybe he was numb inside.

Maybe it was a fourteen year old boy's prank gone heartbreakingly wrong.

'Nothing could have been that bad,' I said to myself, *"if only he'd have told somebody his problems, it never would have ended like this. If only he could have resisted the temptation to give up hope."*

I decided it was time to walk home and face the music, my parents could throw anything they wanted at me this time, I no longer cared.

I walked in and saw them through the obscure glass in the living room door. They jumped to their feet and rushed to give me the telling off of my life.

"Well I can't fucking wait to hear this one," said my dad. "You'd better get your backside in there." He pushed open the door to reveal the chair in the centre of the room again. At least he was confident I was coming home.

"Just let her talk Jim," said my mum, who genuinely looked relieved I was home.

I sat on the interrogation chair and my dad fired questions at me.

"I went for a walk," I said. "I just needed a bit of space." I thought back to what Bernie had suggested and decided to try it out.

"I'm being bullied at school."

I couldn't make eye contact with them, my dad would know I was lying. I was almost as good as him when it came to recognizing bullshit but he was still better.

"Really?" he said, "It's just I've spoken to your school and I asked them if bullying might have been the cause. Guess what they said?"

I shrugged, knowing it probably wouldn't coincide with my story.

"Well, after your teacher had stopped laughing Moll, she told me that you're the biggest bully she's ever known."

"She's one of the reasons I missed school today," I said, "she's awful to me all the time."

I wasn't lying either. I remember sneaking into my classroom one dinner time to play on the grand

piano, I had quite an audience until Mrs Howe came
storming into the room and tore me away from the
thing. She even offered to 'wipe the smirk off my
face' while demanding to know why I'd sneaked in
without her permission.
Even my mum agreed that Mrs Howe was a
miserable old cow. She used to teach my mum
when she was at school and never liked her. That's
how old and bitter she was.

"You know, we even rang Bernie to ask if he'd
seen you. The poor bloke went out of his way to
help us find you. He didn't have to you know, you
don't deserve to have people like that in your life.
You're toxic to everybody you come into contact
with."

The interrogation continued late into the night
until I angled the conversation towards my dad's
favourite subject – 'why are we here?'
He was obsessed with the universe, he believed in
aliens and would talk for hours and hours about his
theories, though never coming to a satisfactory
conclusion.
I'd learned to use this to my advantage to take the
heat off me, it was like throwing a stick for a dog
and it worked every time.
Into the early hours of the morning, he ruminated
whilst watching his dirty women dancing around
half naked on the television.

Chapter Thirteen.

Whilst I was pleased to be getting more space by sharing a room with Beth, she had her silly friends over a lot and it annoyed me.
I went upstairs one day from doing my chores to find one of them sitting on my bed. I had so little privacy anyway that I lost my temper and shouted for her to *move* or *leave*.

"I was just sitting on it." said one of them. "Since when did that become a crime?"
She got up anyway but I was sick of how frequently it was occurring and decided it was time to do something about it.
I went downstairs to the outhouse and looked for my dad's yellow insulation tape, then I went back upstairs and used the tape to divide the room in half.

"If anybody crosses over to my side again, they're going to get a slap." I said, as I sat down on my bed.

"But the door is on your side." Beth looked anxious and her friends didn't know where to look.

"Yes, it is. You should have thought about that though, rules are rules. Looks like you're all staying here then." I laughed.
Beth shouted to my dad, who came charging up the stairs to give me a good telling off and a lecture about bullying.
I was no longer scared of him, I told him I wasn't interested in his woodland walks anymore and refused to go anywhere with him. I'd lost every bit of respect I ever had for him.

Beth's friends stopped coming over as much after that incident.

My mum got a job at the hospital which meant we got to see her a lot more. She seemed a little happier and even taught me how to use the computer she'd bought with her higher wages. I found Encarta to be particularly useful when it came to homework. I'd print out sheets of information and hand it in. My physics teacher gave me an 'E for effort.' I always enjoyed the practical lessons; it was the reading from the board that I struggled with, so I just gave up and told myself I'd research it when I was older.

Bernie, continued to pick me up and drop me home after training. Each time I'd come home just that little bit later because he'd park down that same country lane just outside the town. I began to dread home times when he'd climb into the back seat with me.

The country lane drives stopped abruptly, when on the last occasion, a police officer walked up to the car and tapped onto the window. I suppose he thought we were a couple and he didn't even look at me else he'd have seen how young I was. He told Bernie to move on, that if he saw his car parked there again, then there'd be action taken next time because he'd taken his number plate down. It was the martial arts and the family atmosphere I was addicted to. I was also addicted to the attention

Bernie showed me; he made me feel special, though I didn't enjoy the physical contact at all.

He promised me that one day, I would be running my own classes because he planned to make me an instructor. I didn't want to mess up my chances so I just went along with whatever it was that he wanted.

After I'd given up learning at school, I'd sneak off to the music room and find a piano until one of the teachers would kick me off, sending me back to my lesson. I hadn't been diagnosed with having OCD at the time, but found music to be the thing that calmed me.

Religious Education was probably my least favourite lesson. I told my teacher that I had a right to refuse it because I didn't believe in God. The school informed me that they had a legal right to teach me.

I hated that the foundations of every school I'd ever attended were based upon religion.

My R.E. teacher hated my attendance more than I did because I'd bombard her with questions and provide my own scientific explanations.

I'd never dream of ridiculing somebody for their religious beliefs, everybody has a right to believe in something, I just didn't appreciate it being pushed upon me.

Some of the children had really taken to it and once when my friend, Lindsey, checked herself into the medical room with 'ladies problems', two girls from the class stood over her and prayed to God, that he 'take away the evil inside of her.'

I honestly thought I was going to piss my pants as I stood in the doorway with the crowd I'd managed to gather together.

I'd found a legitimate way to skip lessons. I'd been seeing the school counsellor for a while. His office was in the vicarage on the school grounds. So long as I had that yellow 'get out of jail free' slip in my hand, I could leave whenever I wanted with no questions asked.

The counsellor paid particular interest to my case. He asked me a question and I'd answer with a question. We'd talk about my dad and he'd take notes and give me my options which I'd ignore. I told him I didn't want anything taking further and I just wanted someone to talk to. He promised he wouldn't tell a soul unless I told him otherwise. He said I should write my feelings down, and he sent me away with some blue paper.

I took that paper home with me and wrote a long letter to Bernie. It was eight double sided pages and it included my thoughts and complaints about my family.

I was going to give it to him on Friday after class, in the meantime, I stored it under my bed between the pages of a book.

Unfortunately my sister, Beth, had been snooping through my things and came across it. She gave it to my dad.

Because of my carelessness and her snooping, my life would take a dramatic turn for the worst that day.

Chapter Fourteen.
(Two Weeks Before My Sixteenth Birthday)

I should have taken it as a sign but I missed it completely.

I'm going to divulge an incident that I'm incredibly ashamed of; a moment born of selfishness and self-preservation.

I was going out of my mind with boredom because true to his word, my dad banned me from leaving the house when my younger sister, Beth, wasn't available to babysit me.

Like everybody else in my family, I was counting down the days until I'd be walking out the door. To make it a little easier on myself, I did as I was told and tried to convince my parents that I could behave well. I was hoping they would grant me a short time out of the house.

I intended to get in contact with Bernie at the first available opportunity.

I told them that I'd accepted Bernie, and training, were now in my past, and that I was ready to move forwards with my life.

My parents said that they'd reported Bernie to the police and had tried to make me a 'Ward of Court.' I was a little confused that I'd not once seen a police officer or been given an interview, nor had I seen any evidence that they were looking to surrender their parental responsibility to a judge.

Because of my new grown up attitude, they granted me a day out at the cinema with Beth and

Lou. We were supposed to watch Armageddon, but I had other plans that didn't involve sitting in front of a large screen, listening to people eat popcorn with their mouths open.

I checked the film times, and whilst everybody was in the garden, I called Bernie from the landline and told him to meet me in the park near the bandstand. I knew the phone bill wouldn't be arriving until after my sixteenth birthday because we'd not long had it. I deleted the last number I'd dialled to prevent any comeback.

"I'll be damned if I'm sitting thorough that film," I told my sister. "Why don't you and Lou go watch it on your own and I'll watch something else?"

I think Beth was so excited at the prospect of doing something grown up with her best friend, that she seemed to completely forget she was supposed to be keeping an eye on me.

I told them I'd be waiting outside for them when they came out of the cinema, and they disappeared inside without a second thought.

I walked to the park in the town centre to meet Bernie, and I sat down on a bench. I was fifteen minutes early so I was just killing time.

A foreign woman sat on the seat next to me which I thought annoying and rude as there were plenty of vacant benches nearby.

Then from nowhere, she started to cry desperately, almost wailing.

I felt incredibly awkward,.I didn't know how to comfort her or people in general. I couldn't even bring myself to put my arm around her. It was alien to me.

"Are you okay?" I asked. It seemed such a silly question when she blatantly wasn't, but I felt I was making an effort at least. She explained that her son in law had been attacking and continually raping her for the last four years.

I was speechless, the first selfish thought that entered my head, was that this lady was going to make me late meeting Bernie. She'd suddenly become a burden on my time.

"You need to go to the police station," I told her. "They'll be able to help you there."

I gave her the directions and she even thanked me!

"Look, I have to go, I'm meeting somebody," I said, as I looked at my watch. "I hope you'll be okay."

She thanked me again and walked off in the wrong direction.

There was a part of me at the time that knew I had to take the lady to the police station, there was also part of me that told me she was an adult and was capable of doing it herself. I didn't evaluate her situation with any thought or care, because likely, talking to a stranger would have been a lot easier than being interviewed at the station.

I met Bernie at the bandstand but thoughts of the old lady haunted me. I felt ashamed that I'd been so quick to dismiss her. I told Bernie what had happened and he said it was 'perfectly normal' and that I should be looking out for myself because my need was greater.

"I've found us a place in Peterborough," he said. "It has a garden, we even have our own tree. You're going to love it. Less than a week to go now."
I smiled, but inside I was hurting.
I'll never know whether that sweet old lady made it to the police station to report her son in law, I wish desperately that I'd have escorted her, but at the time, I was out for myself and nobody else. If I didn't meet Bernie, I wouldn't be able to arrange my escape from home. I put my own selfish needs first.

"John, said he'll keep you updated with everything. He's going to ask his mum to pick you up on your birthday and I'll get you from their house. The club just isn't the same without you. Loads of people have left. I told them I'd still be coming back on Fridays and the odd Tuesday, but they seem to have given up."
Less than a week and my ordeal at home would be over, Bernie had promised to make me an instructor. I was looking forward to my new life. He was an adult, he'd look out for me.

"You'd better get back now in case your dad is out spying on you, you know what he's like."

I wouldn't have put it past him, he spied on everyone. The only reason I used the home phone was because his recording device was broken. He used to record every conversation that was made from the house.

137

I met Beth, and Lou, outside the cinema. Their eyes blinked wildly as they adjusted to the daylight. I asked them to brief me about the film on the walk home, in case my dad decided to question me about it later to make sure I'd been.

Fortunately, he never brought it up; he was barely talking to me since I'd admitted my situation with Bernie. Beth didn't mention that I'd gone off on my own. I think she realised she'd get in just as much trouble as me.

Because I'd gotten away with it, I began to get brave and a little carefree. When you become carefree - it's easier to slip up.

I persuaded my mum to let me go to another martial arts class. It was taught by Brian, who was a friend of Bernie's. She gave me the benefit of the doubt and let me go. It was taught on Tuesday's like the other club I'd been to.

She got my brother to drop me off in his car, and I waved as he watched me walk towards the door before driving off.

I didn't go inside. Instead, I walked up to Bernie's class around the corner which was in full swing. As I walked through the door, it was pure coincidence that Bernie was in the hallway. He turned pale when I caught his attention.

"What are you doing here, Petal?" he asked, as he ushered me gently outside. "If anybody catches you here then you'll get yourself, and me, in trouble, everything will be ruined. You won't be able to move out because your parent will stop you

138

leaving. If you keep sneaking off they'll call the police and they'll lock you up."

I couldn't understand why it was such a big secret. Why couldn't Bernie just apply for custody of me until I was old enough to leave home? Was I really doing something so wrong that I had to sneak about everywhere?

"How did you get out the house anyway? Are they letting you out now?"

"Kind of, I'm supposed to be at Brian's class tonight."

"Well if you hang about until this class is finished, I can speak to you then. I've got something for you anyway," he said, tapping his nose.

"Okay." I said, as I sat down in a chair.

"What are you doing? You can't wait around here. Go and keep yourself entertained for the next hour, *then* come back."

I sat behind some large charity donation bins in the car park opposite, and I waited until the class was finished.

When I saw people leaving, I was relieved, I had enough time to speak to Bernie and get back to Brian's class before my brother arrived to pick me up. To my horror, Bernie had decided to drop some of his students off after the class.

It was about fifteen minutes later when he pulled up outside the building again. He got out the car and led me inside.

"I've found a community centre in Peterborough," he smiled. "It's where I'm going to run the new classes from once I'm over there."

"What's it like?" I asked.

"It's a little bigger than this hall and it's cheaper. I've already put an advert in the local paper, and I've had loads of interest already."

He reached into his pocket and produced a small blue leather book that looked like a passport. It had my name and my new address written inside. It just needed my photograph adding.

"Can you guess what this is?" he asked, waving it about in front of my face. "Told you I'd make you an instructor." It was my license to teach.

Everything suddenly became very real, and I could see my new life taking form.

"You need to do one thing though, Petal."

"What's that?"

"You need to promise me that you're definitely going to move in with me, because I've spent a fortune on getting you registered."

He held the little blue book in his hand as his tone became more serious. I couldn't take my eyes off of it.

"Also, there are conditions if you're going to be teaching."

I couldn't understand why there would be conditions, I was a registered instructor with the British Kickboxing Association now.

"You'll have to train really hard, you'll have your own class but you'll be teaching children. The classes will start an hour before the adult class. You do understand you won't be teaching the adult classes straight away don't you?" I nodded my head, though I was a little disappointed.

"I'll be in touch with you via John, this week, remember, don't tell a soul about the engagement or that you're going to be running your own classes else you'll mess it all up for yourself. Understand?"

"Yes, I won't say a word." I replied.

"Okay, I'll have to keep this with me," he stuffed my instructor's license back into his pocket. "You can have it when you're in Peterborough okay?" I nodded again.

"Right, you'd better get back to Brian's class now before your parents find out you didn't go." I looked at my watch; I should have left ten minutes ago to guarantee getting back before I'd be picked up. I was late, but I wouldn't panic, not in front of Bernie. I had to show him I was an adult and could deal with difficult situations else he might change his mind about me moving away with him. I was sure Bernie would drop me off, a fifteen minute walk for me would be less than five minutes in the car. Even if he just dropped me on the corner, I would have been able to sneak into the class.

"I don't suppose you could give me a lift to Brian's class could you? It's just that I'm going to be late otherwise."

"I'd love to, Petal, but I have to go to Barbara's house now to collect the rest of my things." My heart sank, he would have been driving near Brian's class anyway to get to his ex's house. I could feel the panic creeping up on me again.

"Okay, I have to go now then because I'm late already."

"Okay Petal, stay safe eh?"

I wanted to run like the wind but I was worried people would look at me and think I was a little strange, so I just walked as quickly as I could instead.

My fears were confirmed as I approached the building and saw my brother's car parked right outside the entrance. Because it was dark, I decided I'd try and sneak around the back of the building and walk around the other side to make it look as though I'd used a different exit. It was shrouded by trees and would give me plenty of cover.

That plan failed the moment I saw my mum walking out of the building looking very angry. I could faintly hear her cursing my name. She must have been in and spoken to Brian, he would have told her I'd not been there all night. I could imagine the conversation.

"Oh my god," I said under my breath. "Please don't let me be in trouble for anything at all, please, please, please, please." I muttered, repeating my ritual. I was glad there was nobody immediately near because they would have thought I was crazy. I felt crazy for sure.

She caught sight of me as I stood on the corner and shouted at me to 'get the fuck over here'.

I couldn't wriggle out of this one; I'd run out of ideas.

She looked calm as I approached the car. I tried to do so with ease, for fear would have had me running in the opposite direction.

She almost flew towards me and took hold of my hair, pushing me into the car before I could even say a word.

"You lying little bitch." she hissed. "We got here early because we knew you'd do something like this. Beth told us what happened at the cinema. You really are a devious little shit aren't you? Just wait until you get home."

We drove back and I remember the hateful look my brother gave me in the rear view mirror. That was it, I was definitely going to move out when I turned sixteen: everybody hated me.

"You've been with him again haven't you?" she shouted. "Get inside that fucking house now."

I thought I'd at least be safe on the driveway, she wouldn't shout in public because she was always worried about what the neighbours thought. But she was past caring.

She threw me in the house by my hair again.

"Get up to your fucking room now! I swear to god, if you go near that pervert again then we'll call the police and he'll rot in prison," she screamed, as the spectators gathered to watch me slowly vanish up the stairs.

I lay down in my bedroom that I shared with Beth. She was up there too. I couldn't blame any of this on her, it was my own doing, she'd just been an accessory.

"They caught you out too then?" I whispered, as I noticed blood from my scalp caused by the hair pulling incident.

"Yeah, I'm grounded now."

"For how long?"

"Forever, I think."

I turned off the light and got into bed.

"What the hell is that?" Beth whispered.

"What the hell is what?"

"Quick, put the light on. Quick!"

I flicked it back on.

"Look at the size of it," she whispered. "I can't sleep in here tonight, you know I'm scared of them."

On the wall was the biggest spider we'd ever seen. There would be no point shouting my dad to take it out because we were both in too much trouble. There were no glasses upstairs to remove it, and killing the critter would have been too noisy and we were forbidden to kill spiders anyway. My dad always said that if he ever caught us killing one, that he'd stamp on us too, to see how we liked it.

We had a similar issue in our bedroom a few months before. There was a spider's nest in the corner above my bed, and I begged my dad to get rid of it, or to at least let me vacuum it up. He declined though and I'll never forget the day they hatched out. I'd woken up during the night covered in tiny translucent baby spiders, crawling all over the duvet and in my hair.

"We'll swap beds," I said. "I'm not going to catch the bloody thing, it'll probably bite me. It looks like a biter."

I prepared myself, dressing head to toe and tucking everything in so it couldn't crawl on my skin if it climbed into the bed. It was the worst night's sleep I'd ever had, and to make matters worse, my dad came into our bedroom around three in the morning. He stood in the doorway before turning on the light.

"She's at it again!" he shouted, as my mum came running. "You're not going to believe this!"

"What?" she asked, as she stumbled sleepily into the bedroom.

"She's dressed! The little bitch is planning to run away in the middle of the night. Well we caught you out this time didn't we? I suggest you get your fucking pyjamas on now!"

They took all my clothes out of the bedroom and slammed the door behind them. Beth was still fast asleep in bed, I didn't want to wake her up, she'd already been punished enough because of me.

As I drifted back off to sleep, something my mum had said earlier ran through my mind. She'd said that if I ever saw Bernie again, they would call the police. This meant that they hadn't been to the police. I doubted it all along but now I knew for sure. Why would they? Their own parenting would have been thrown into question because I'd have told the police exactly what my parents were like. They would implicate themselves.

Chapter Fifteen.
(The next day in Peterborough)

"You need to find something to wear that makes you look a little bit older," said Bernie, as he rifled through my bin liners. "Try this blazer."
He threw me the red velvet blazer that Beryl had handed down to me. As I put it on over my purple lace top, I could still smell my mums' perfume on it that Beryl used to borrow. Having no fashion sense whatsoever, I teamed it with a pair of pale blue suede trousers, (such as was the fashion in the late nineties, [or so I thought.])

"Yes, I think that will do. You'll easily pass for nineteen if anybody asks you okay, Petal?"
I nodded my head and waited for him to leave the room so I could get changed, but it hit me that he thought he was in a relationship and I'd have to get changed in front of him.

"You should wear your hair up too, it makes you look older, so I used to read in Lou's magazines."
I nodded again and pulled my long hair back into a ponytail.

"Now, my parents are really nice and if you're polite to them and say what I tell you to say, you'll win them over no problem. You'll only get one chance to make a first impression with them though so make an effort okay?"
I nodded again.

"Well smile then."
I did but inside I was screaming.

We got into the car and headed towards Werrington, which was a couple of miles away.

It was a very grand, very immaculate garden that we walked through to reach the front door. It terrified me that it would be the same inside and I was right.

"This is Moll," said Bernie, as we walked through to the living room. "She's one of my students from the club."

His parents eyed me suspiciously as I looked around their massive living room. They must have both been in their early seventies.

"Right, I'm going to pop over the road and see Eric, I haven't seen him for nearly ten years would you believe? I want to see if he's still got my step ladders."

Then he left.

"Have a seat," said his mum, slowly pointing at an armchair opposite Bernie's dad who sat there like a beached whale.

Bernie left me in that house with them for over half an hour as they pelted me with questions. Asking me who I really was? Did my parents know I was out so late? And what time was I going home?

"I'm not going home." I told her.

"Well you can't live with Bernie dear, he's living with Barbara." She laughed.

"Not anymore he doesn't," I replied.

"I think I'd know if my own son had split up with Barbara thank you very much," she said, as she became more hostile. "And how old did you say you were again?"

"Nineteen."

"Really? It's just that you don't look a day over fifteen. Please dear god tell me you're at least sixteen."

"I'm nineteen." I insisted.

"Then what's your date of birth, dear?"
My date of birth? I searched my brain for my date of birth but it had shut down through fear and denied me access. I only had to minus three years from my actual date of birth and I'd have wriggled out of the situation.

"It's just that you don't appear too sure, dear that's all. Why don't you give me your mums' number and I'll give her a ring."

"I've left home," I told her. "I'm not going back there."

"What?" she raised the volume of her voice a little. "This is wrong, if you're nineteen then why can't you tell me your date of birth?"

"It was my birthday yesterday." I replied.

"That isn't what I asked. What year were you born?"
She could tell I was making it up and trying to bide my time for Bernie to come back. I couldn't bare the questions and eventually: I told her the truth, that I was sixteen. I felt so ashamed of my age.

I heard Bernie whistling as he came through the kitchen, but the whistling stopped as he saw their faces.

"I need to speak to you in private," she said, as she directed him towards the kitchen, slamming the door behind them. Then the shouting started.

Bernie's dad hadn't said a word to me since I arrived, he sat opposite in a big armchair that held his weight and he stared directly at my face.

"So how long has this been going on for?" He asked.

I didn't give him an answer because as far as I was concerned: I didn't have to. He was just a stranger to me.

"I mean, how old were you when this all started? Were you underage?" He smiled sickeningly from behind his large framed glasses.

Nothing could have prepared me for what he said next.

"Like older men do you?" he lowered his voice, "Then how about sorting out an old man like me? I'll pay you."

I felt disgusted, and about two feet tall at that moment. The disgusting, fat bastard sat opposite me grinning wildly whilst he put his hand down the front of his trousers to touch himself.

"You can come round here anytime you want. She doesn't understand me, you see. But I'll look after you, don't you worry about that."

I ignored him. He hid behind the fact he was a pensioner so there was nothing really I could do. If I told Bernie, he probably wouldn't believe me.

"Don't you worry, you'll never have to look at me again because I'm going," shouted Bernie, as he stormed back into the room.

"Come on, we're off. We're not wanted around here," he said, and I was just glad to be getting out of there.

I followed him out of the living room and back through the kitchen as he yelled more abuse at his mum. His dad followed behind me and ran his fingers up and down my back until his fingers stopped on my backside.

His mum was crying and pleading with him to do the right thing and go back to Barbara, but he callously told her to 'stick it'.

I felt as though his dad had tainted me when he touched me, as I could feel it for a long time afterwards, almost as if he'd left a scar. There was an actual physical sensation of coldness on my back for a while after.

Bernie was in a foul mood as we drove back to the caravan, and he didn't speak a word to me until we pulled up outside. I was overcome with anxiety. At least when my dad was angry with me, I kind of knew what to expect.

"Why didn't you tell them you were nineteen like I said?" His voice was calm but he didn't look at me.

"I did, but she kept asking me questions."

"She?" he shouted. "That 'she' you're referring to, is my mother, I fucking told you what to say if they asked you. It wasn't difficult, was it?"

His face was frozen in an expression I'd never seen before and it scared me.

"Your mum wouldn't believe me, I really tried to tell her."

"Well you didn't try hard enough then did you because she's at home crying now, they want

nothing to do with me and it's all your fucking fault because you don't do as you're told."
I hung my head in shame and didn't know what to say.

"Is it because your own parents don't want you anymore, is that it? Are you that bitter and twisted that you'd try to destroy my relationship with my own parents? Is this your way of punishing me little girl?"
I shook my head as I sobbed.

"I made a mistake bringing you here, you've only been here two days and already you've turned my life upside down on its arse. I'm taking you back to your parents."
I pleaded with him not to take me back, I couldn't go back to living there. I imagined their faces if I were to turn up on their door step, my life would be unbearable. I cried hysterically until I almost hyperventilated, finally he agreed I could stay.

"Just don't play your fucking games with me you little bitch because you'll see a whole different side of me and you won't like it."
He pushed my head with force and it slammed into the passenger window. I didn't dare check whether the warm sensation on my face was blood, but the taste confirmed it when it reached my mouth.
He sat quietly for a minute as he collected his thoughts.

"And what did my dad have to say about it all when I was in the kitchen?" He studied my face.

I froze up when he mentioned his dad. I wouldn't be able to tell him what happened because he'd be furious. I started to cry again.

"You fucking tell me what he said. Did he try it on with you?"
Then it clicked that this had probably happened before, why else would he have mentioned something so specific? Before I could say another word, he lost his temper again.

"Well fucking answer me." He shouted.
I nodded my head.

"I knew it, I just knew it. Every bloody time."
Before I could say anything, he walked into the house and called his parents. I followed slowly behind.

"Yes it's me, I don't care if you don't want to talk to me, I suggest you put Dad on the phone now."
He paused.

"I couldn't care less if he doesn't want to talk to me. Tell him if he doesn't come to the phone now, then I'll just have you repeat everything back to him."
After another pause, the tone of his voice changed. It was cold and calculated.

"You disgusting old bastard," he spat. "You couldn't help yourself could you? You've been doing this to me for years," he paused, and gave me an icy stare. "You'll be lucky if I don't tell Mum what you're really like. It'd kill her, you know that? I'm not going to but it's for her - not you. You're dead to me do you understand?"

152

Then he slammed down the phone and it bounced off its rest.

"You," he said, as he pointed at me. "You just stay out of my way tonight or you'll regret it."
He walked into the bedroom and the walls rattled as he slammed the door.
I slept on one of the plastic garden chairs that night.

Chapter Sixteen.

Bernie had been offered some factory work, and although he had an engineering degree, he took a production line job: packing electrical components into boxes. He despised it.

"You need to get a job, or get yourself into school. The choice is yours," he said. "I'm not going to support you financially for sitting around on your arse."

He picked up the yellow pages and threw it at me. "You'd better be enrolled by the time I get home else there's going to be trouble."

He slammed the door as he walked out and the walls rattled again.

I didn't know what to do; look for local schools in the yellow pages and ring them up? I'd never had to do that before, my mum dealt with those things.

I searched under 'schools' and found one that was relatively nearby, a couple of miles walk at best. I picked up the phone and dialled the number.

"Hello, Hereward Community College?"

"Oh, Hi," I cleared my throat. "I'm looking to enrol myself at your school. How would I go about doing that?"

"Enrol yourself?"

"Yes."

"Well, erm, how old are you?"

"I'm sixteen." I said, crossing my fingers and thinking about endure the wrath of Bernie if she couldn't sort it out for me right at that moment."

"And what's your name dear?" I could hear her tapping away on her keyboard.

"Moll."

"Okay, Moll, could you put your parents on the phone please? It's just that I've never heard of a pupil enrolling themselves before."

"I moved out," I told her. "I don't have any contact with my parents anymore."

"Okay, Moll, give me a minute, I'm just going to see if I can get hold of the head teacher. I'm not sure how to handle this. Won't be a moment Okay?"

Ugh, I didn't like head teachers. The only time I'd ever spoken to one was when I'd been in trouble. I associated them with my wrong doings. It sounded as though she'd transferred my call as I heard another ring. The cheek! Why couldn't she have dealt with it there and then for me? Why did she need to put me through to the head?
My heart began to race again, I didn't know how to talk to adults. What the hell was I doing?

"Hello?"

"Erm hello," I said, "I'm looking to enrol myself at your school."
I didn't feel confident anyway but speaking to the head teacher made me incredibly nervous. I was expecting to be told off again. I prayed he wouldn't dismiss me.

"This is quite an exceptional case, Moll, I've never had a student enrol themselves before.

Students are around thirteen years of age when they start at our school, I suppose that's why."

"So can I join your school?" I asked.

"Look, I really need to meet you first. Are you living on your own?"

"No, I'm staying with a friend."
It was all I could think of, had I said 'my fiancé' it would have raised questions. The term 'fiancé' turned my stomach anyway.

"Okay, are you free to come in today? I'll be available until about half past ten, come any time before then."
I said goodbye and hung up the phone. I'd forgotten to ask for directions. I felt sick, how on earth was I supposed to get there by half past ten when I didn't know where I was going? I didn't have access to the internet at the time; it wasn't as widely accessible by my generation at that time.

I went into the bedroom and started to look through Bernie's things, surely he had a map of Peterborough somewhere? Then I thought, why would he have a map of Peterborough? He grew up here, even if he did have a map, it would be in the car.
There was a petrol station down the road, I decided I'd have to go there, however, Bernie hadn't left me any money so I couldn't buy one.
I got myself dressed into the same outfit I wore when I'd met Bernie's parents, it was all I had that made me look presentable. I tied back my hair again and found myself a pen and paper.

My heeled shoes were beginning to look tatty and they were quite difficult to walk in too.

I got myself together and walked towards the petrol station, I'd just have a little look inside the maps, I told myself. I had no choice.

I'd taken a notepad and pen with me so I could write down the directions to the school. After a couple of minutes of browsing, I began to take notes.

"It isn't a library you know, love. If you're not going to buy it, then don't touch it," said a greasy man, who sat at the cash register.

I was hideously embarrassed and legged it out of there.

"You're a stray aren't you?" he laughed, as I let the door swing behind me.

I'd taken enough notes to get me a couple of streets in the right direction, I would be in the right area at least, or so I thought. The streets were full of council houses and I was a little lost. The sound of a dog barking distracted me.

Because my eyesight was still terrible, I had to walk right up to the street signs to read them. I must have looked very strange constantly crossing over the road. I didn't want to look lost, not in that area, I'd heard it wasn't a pleasant one.

By ten o'clock I'd found the school. It looked run down and shabby, the theme of everything in my life at the time.

'This is it', I told myself. *'If you walk through this door, you've made a life for yourself here. There'll be no turning back once you're in school again.'*

The reception area was marginally warmer than outside and a young looking lady sat behind the desk. I hated the smell of schools.

"Are you late?" she asked, with a stern voice.

"I'm not a pupil here, I've come to enrol myself today. The head teacher said he'd see me before half past ten."

She looked at the clock.

"You should have been here ages ago then shouldn't you? He might not be able to see you now. Take a seat."

She gestured towards a very formal sitting area, a couple of students sniggered as they walked past. I didn't look very old at all, yet I was dressed in these ridiculous adult clothes. I felt very self-conscious.

"You're lucky, he'll see you now. Please wait there and he'll come through to get you."

The only thing that stopped me getting up and walking out was the thought of having to tell Bernie that I couldn't find a school. It would be over soon enough, I told myself. I estimated how long the meeting should take. Twenty minutes at a push perhaps? In twenty long painful minutes it would all be over and I could walk out of the building back to the safety of my own company.

"Hello Moll," said the head teacher, as he came through a set of double doors. "It's nice to meet you, follow me through this way."

He let me through a labyrinth of classrooms and corridors, my concerns now became not of the enrolment; but how I would get back out of the building. Even if I could remember the order of corridors, my eyesight was terrible. I couldn't see the other children staring at me, but I could feel it.

"Have a seat Moll."

I sat on a chair that was considerably smaller than his. I was facing the window and though it was cold outside; the autumn sun shone brightly through the windows. All I could see was the silhouette of his head. It took me back and reminded me of my dad and my heart began to race.

"Don't look so nervous, you're not in any trouble," he said gently. "Here, let me close these blinds a little, that sun is right in your eyes." He turned the stick slightly and suddenly I could see his face properly.

"Now look Moll, your case concerns me. You say you've left home, yet you've only just turned sixteen. You say you're living with a friend, I find that difficult to believe," he paused. "So here's what I'll do. If you give me your parents home number, I'll ring them to find out what's been going on."

"Do you have to ring them?" I asked, my mouth dry.

"Yes, I need their consent if you want to study here. I know you're sixteen but you're not an adult yet. It's our policy. Well, it isn't but I've just made it policy. I'm just looking out for you. I know you won't like it but I'm a parent myself you know."

'Oh bugger', I thought. I hadn't spoken to my parents since the day I walked out. I tried to weigh up the pros and con's whilst the head teacher waited on me. My parents couldn't do any harm on the

other end of the line. Bernie could do far more damage to me if I didn't get myself signed up.

I looked at my watch, ten minutes to go and then my twenty minutes would be up. It was useful knowing that he had to be somewhere at half past ten. My ordeal would have definitely been over by then.

I gave him my parents number and sat back to watch with a feeling that everything was out of control again.

'They can't hurt me from the end of the line', I told myself over again.

"Hello, is this Moll's parents? Okay, don't worry, there's nothing wrong with her. She's come into my school today wanting to enrol herself. I just wanted to check that you knew about all of this because she isn't from around here, is she?"

He paused for a short while and eyed me carefully.

"I see. Yes, I understand."

He gave them his own personal number they'd be able to contact him on anytime. He hung up the phone and sighed. It wasn't a good sigh either.

"Don't you think you should go back to your parents?" he asked, as he rubbed his forehead. "It's just that I don't think your situation is ideal at all."

I didn't ask him what they'd said, I didn't want to know. It was obvious they'd told him about Bernie.

"Look, even if you think they don't care, I'm sure deep down somewhere they do. It's in a parent's nature."

"Nothing comes natural to them." I said, "I'm not going back home. If you're not going to give me

160

a place at your school then say now and I can look for somewhere else. My parents are evil."

"I didn't say I wasn't going to give you a place," he sighed again. "You're not going to fit in well at all. I'm going to put you in the sixth form and you can re-sit your GCSE's. That's about all I can do to accommodate you though."

"Why do you think I won't fit in?" I asked.

"Because you're living with a reasonable amount of independence, you won't fit in back in year eleven. It's sixth form or nothing."

"Yes, I'll take it." I hadn't even sat my first lot of GCSE's.

"Okay, ask for some forms on your way out and bring them back in with you tomorrow when you start."

"Tomorrow?"

"Yes, you start at 8:45. Don't let me regret this will you? I just don't want this type of thing glamorized that's all."

There wasn't any chance of that happening. I planned to tell nobody about Bernie. I was ashamed.

"I'll take you on a quick tour of the common room if you like, introduce you to your class. It'll only be a quick walk through though because I have somewhere to be soon."

I felt indifferent after leaving, I'd managed to get back into school which meant Bernie wouldn't be able to moan at me about it. The idea of starting the next day terrified me. I wouldn't know anybody, there was no school uniform either so I had to make do with whatever I could find. Bernie wouldn't buy me any new clothes; he insisted I didn't need them.

"What the fuck is this?" said Bernie, when he came in from work. "You know I can't stand the sight of the stuff."
Bernie was a vegetarian and I was still a meat eater; I'd made him a casserole and I had prepared myself something else.
"Did you carry it all back in the same bag? You did, didn't you?"
I denied it and said that the meat was in a separate bag. They were only burgers in a box afterall.
"If I find out you're lying... I'll give you one more chance. Were they in the same bag together or not?"
"No," I insisted.
He went through the cupboard and pulled out an Asda bag, there was only one left.
"You lying whore! Why did you fucking lie about it?"
"I didn't, the other bag is in the bin outside." I said.
He sent me outside to get it for him and I looked through the wheelie bin for one.
"You'd better get back in here now, you're a fucking liar. I'm not eating this shit, are you trying to poison me?"
"It hasn't got any meat in it." I said.
"I don't fucking care." He picked up the plate of hot casserole and threw it at me. It was my scalp that burned the most, but thankfully I was wearing a

blazer and other than a little that landed on my hand, I was relatively scald free.

I went into the bathroom and began picking pieces of soft carrot out of my hair, it squashed under the pressure of my fingers which made it difficult to remove; the gravy was beginning to set hard in my hair.

He stood in the doorway and his tone changed.

"Get your coat, we're going out for dinner. Don't worry about the casserole."

I sorted out my hair out as best I could, though I now smelt like a stew.

We got into Bernie's car and headed to an Indian restaurant on Lincoln Road. The food was really quite nice and Bernie was really nice to me also. I'd ordered a biryani for vegetarians. Bernie, said I could order anything I wanted but I played it safe.

"I've just got to nip out to the car, Moll," he said. "I've left my bloody wallet in there. I won't be a minute, Petal, okay?"

He'd parked in Kwik Save car park just around the corner, and I watched as he walked past the window without looking at me. He still had that stupid bounce when he walked.

The waiter brought over some after dinner mints and the bill.

"He's just gone to get his wallet," I said.

I waited for almost an hour and Bernie didn't come back. He'd left me there on my own, about an hour's walk home in the growing darkness.

The waiter looked concerned and began muttering something to a person I assumed was the manager. They both came over to the table.

"What's happening? It's been nearly an hour, is he coming back to pay for this meal or not?"
"I don't know," I shrugged. "Can I just nip around the corner and see if he's still there?"

"You can't leave," said the waiter. "You have to pay for your meal."

"I don't have any money to pay for it," I said, trying to hold back my tears. My face was now burning in a similar way to my scalp. "I'm sure he'll be back if you don't mind waiting a little bit longer."

"Well, where is he parked?"

"Just around the corner, in the Kwik Save car park," I sniffled.
The waiter looked at the manager and he left the restaurant. He came back a couple of minutes later shaking his head.

"There isn't a single car in the car park. Is there anybody you can call to pick you up? How old are you?"
I wasn't going to hide my true age this time; Bernie didn't know these people and obviously didn't have any respect for them either. I thought my young age would help me in this situation.

"I'm only sixteen," I sobbed. "I don't have anybody I can ring, he doesn't have a phone."
That last part was a lie, the last thing I needed was them ringing Bernie, it would have been almost unbearable for me. I had no idea why he'd left me

there but thought it must have been something really important. Perhaps he was in trouble? I needed to get back and find out.

"And you don't have any money at all?" asked the owner.

I shook my head.

"I'm going to let you get home, because I can't expect you to pay for this yourself. It was clearly some kind of cruel trick," said the owner. "If you can give me your address, and somebody could pop the money in before the end of the week, I'd appreciate it. A favour for a favour, based on trust, eh?"

I agreed and scribbled the address down on one of their compliments slips. I even put Bernie's name on there. I thanked them whole heartedly and began my three mile walk back to the caravan. The sky always seemed overcast in Peterborough, and the rain when it fell, always fell in a miserable fashion. I couldn't appreciate the beauty of St. Peter's Cathedral that I regularly walked past on my many trips to Asda, it seemed to be a landmark to my hideous existence.

Bernie's car was on the driveway when I eventually got back. The lights were on too. I was pissed off but felt more fear than anything else. My anger would have to go on the back burner again. I envisioned myself slamming the door as I entered, and even yelling at him; asking what the hell he was playing at, before packing my things and leaving him. This was only ever a daily fantasy for me though. The reality was that I had nowhere to go and nobody to turn to.

"Maybe you'll learn your lesson next time you silly cow," he said, as he looked up from the computer screen. "We don't have money to waste so the next time you go shopping, *think* about what you're doing."

I couldn't see the point he was trying to make, but I'd never put vegetables and meat in the same bag together again.

"In fact, Moll, you're too stupid to grasp what I'm trying to say, I think it would be better if you became a vegetarian like me."

"But I like meat."

"It isn't up for debate you crazy bitch," he laughed, "while you're under my roof, what I say goes."

I started school the following day. I was incredibly nervous but I felt as though I could reinvent myself and be whatever I wanted to be. They didn't know my past and I didn't have to tell them anything.

I was assigned to girl called 'Stacey' when I entered the common room. It was nothing like my old school, the paint was flaking from the walls, and it was painted like the inside of a hospital. The other children were fascinated with me because I was living independently so to speak. I told them nothing of Bernie.

Stacey followed me around everywhere, and in the first week, she had invited me over to her house every day after school. We'd do normal teenager things like listening to music and apply makeup. I even had an invite to her seventeenth birthday party. I remember exactly what I wore, a long cream satin skirt and a white vest top with a cream crochet jumper over the top. I drank enough taboo and lemonade to make me a tipsy sixteen year old, and I remember running down the main road at twilight with nothing on my feet because I had to get back before Bernie.

He got back before me that day and a massive row erupted because he wanted an invite to the party too. Not only had I not told people about him, it was supposed to be an adult free zone; even Stacey's parents had made themselves scarce. Above all else, I didn't understand why he'd want an invite to a party surrounded by sixteen year old girls, (though I'd soon find out).

Chapter Seventeen.

"This is Tony and Ady from work," he said, as he walked through the door after work the next day. "They're going to be staying for dinner. What have we got in?" He rubbed his hands together and looked at me like I was some kind of idiot.

I'd heard him speak of them before; one of them was South African and apparently had a wicked sense of humour. The other was a lot quieter.

"There isn't any food in really," I said, "well not enough for everyone anyway. We'll need to go to Asda."

"Why didn't you go earlier then? What the fuck have you been doing all day?"

I was going to tell him that I'd been at school all day but I remembered that I was supposed to be nineteen if anybody asked, and he knew it.

"We don't have to stay for dinner if it's a problem," said Tony awkwardly.

"It isn't a problem at all, mate. The only problem around here is this lazy, stupid bitch. She can't do anything right. He pointed at me, "Get your shoes on and take a walk up to Asda while you still have your legs."

I went through to the bedroom and put on my shoes, I could hear Tony talking to Bernie in the living room.

"The point, Tony, is that she lives here and contributes fuck all. I support the lazy bitch and she can't even be arsed to make sure there's enough food for dinner when I get in from work."

"I won't be long," I said.

"You'd better not be, we were supposed to be upgrading the computers after dinner, now we've got to wait for you to get back."

"Why don't you do that while I'm out?" I asked.

"Why don't you do that while I'm out," he mimicked. "Because that wasn't the fucking plan, *that's* why. Just get out of my sight."

Tony looked down at my shoes, it was clear to see that they had become un-bonded on the inside. I'd tried to stick them together with some super glue but it dried white and sticky, every step I took, the sole parted and the glue came un-bonded like parting lips.

"What size shoe are you?" Tony asked, "it's just that you look around the same size as my girlfriend and she probably buys a new pair every week. She's got loads she needs to get rid of. She's a size five."

"I'm a size six, but thanks anyway." I said, my cheeks were burning with shame as I turned to leave.

"Don't forget the wine this time will you?" Bernie shouted after me.

He always mentioned the wine, whether it was to convince his friends I was over eighteen I do not know. It was either Hock, or Leibfraumilch, that he wanted. Of course I was only sixteen and had no chance of getting served. I was underage.

I used to enjoy the walk to Asda, it would take me about forty minutes to get there, and I'd listen to my Club Ninja album on my imitation walkman to pass the time.

Walking back would always be a different matter altogether. I found myself struggling with the weight of the shopping bags sometimes, paired with my shoes that were falling apart, it was distressing to find such discomfort in a simple task like walking.

I tried my luck at Asda again, but the cashier asked for my proof of age. I wondered whether she'd let it pass out of pity just once, if only she knew what I'd be going home to. However, it always ended in humiliation and angry eyes upon me as my lack of identification held up the queue.

It was dark when I got in, the three of them were tinkering with computer parts. They were complaining about their foreman at work, calling him a *fat, greasy cunt.*

I chopped the vegetables in the tiny kitchen, where the ancient, grease ridden cooker had cleaned up to be almost satisfactory.

Since becoming a vegetarian, my diet consisted of vegetables, Beanfeast, and cheap lentil soup. They were the only items allowed on Bernie's list of approved foods. He'd occasionally allow chick peas and kidney beans, but I found them rather bland.

I made the mistake of leaving the living room ajar and I could hear their conversations. I hated how Bernie carried on as though the circumstances were normal. I hated to hear him laugh, it sickened me to my stomach.

Ady told a sick joke, the kind that would twist the very guts of anybody. It was truly chilling and undoubtedly referred to paedophilia and sexually abusing young children.

It was one of the most disgusting things I'd ever heard and I was close to actually throwing up in the sink. I wanted to use my anger and disgust to castrate the disgusting bastard. I had the knife ready in my hand, but again it was just a fantasy. The next most disgusting thing that came was the roar of Bernie's laughter.

I'd learnt to recognize every creak of the floors in the mobile home. They'd warn me if somebody was lurking nearby, if I was being watched, and if somebody was in a bad mood. They alerted me that Bernie had got to his feet and was bouncing with his stupid walk towards the kitchen. I composed myself and pretended I hadn't heard a word.

"Is it ready yet, Petal?" he said, in an almost polite tone. It unnerved me how quickly his personality could switch.

I didn't have dinner with them, Ady, and Tony, sat on the grimy patio chairs and Bernie took one of the rotten kitchen chairs through for himself.

I confined myself to the bathroom, locking the door whilst I ran myself a bath.

The taps were still covered with mildew despite my best efforts to clean them. I continually checked the water to make sure there were no bits floating around. The toilet was encrusted with faeces, and the lino floor was peeling away to reveal years of rot underneath.

I turned up the radio and submerged my body to my shoulders. It was the only place I felt safe to let out my emotions and have a damn good cry, to let the radio drown out my painful, muffled cries.

Sometimes, I'd burrow my face deep into a towel to stifle the noise.

I'd weigh up the pros and cons of going home to my family, but I could never come to a satisfactory conclusion. Guilt and shame ate away from the inside, and on my exterior, I was a mess of cuts and bruises.

'She trains too hard,' Bernie would joke. *'I keep telling her to calm it down a bit in case people think I'm a wife beater.'* This would always follow with raucous laughter, I wasn't his 'wife', I hated him calling me his wife: it made my skin crawl.

"Where's the wine?" he shouted, as he banged on the door.

"I couldn't get any," I said, as I tried to disguise the lump in my throat. I hoped he hadn't heard me clear my throat, he'd know I was nervous. "They wouldn't serve me."

'Did I lock the door?' I said over and over in my head, it was all that separated me from him, all that hid my expression of horror - the thing he fed off. He rattled the handle.

"Why the fuck have you locked the door? I suggest you open it now before I break the damn thing down."

I panicked, but moved quickly, throwing my bathrobe on. The belt that held it closed must have been left in the bedroom as I couldn't find it in my haste. I looked at the tiny window that opened only slightly at the top. Had I been able to climb out of it - I would have.

I opened the door and as the cool air hit my open pores, he grabbed at my hair and pulled me in the direction of the kitchen. We were going to the living room.

He pushed me through the door and my gown fell open, exposing me in front of his friends. My face was red with shame.

"I suggest you apologise to Ady and Tony, they expected a glass of wine with their dinner and once again, you fucked everything up."

"I'm sorry," I said, looking at them from underneath my wet hair strewn across my face.

"Don't worry about it," said Tony, "it's only bloody wine Bernie for crying out loud."

Ady said nothing, but gave me the most disgusting look I'd ever seen. As though I'd served him a plate of actual shit for his dinner.

He launched me back into the kitchen and I ran through to the bathroom to cry. I didn't lock the door though, I knew better than that.

I could hear them shouting in the living room and my heart turned to lead as I knew it was my fault.

"Jesus, Bernie, why did you do that?" I heard Tony shout. I thought he was trying to protect me but it wouldn't last, despite his best efforts.

"Because she's from a fucked up family, *that's* why. She needs some discipline and learn some respect."

Stacey lived on the same road as me, though we were at separate ends. We walked home together every day, though I was always worried she'd try and follow me home one day, to discover I lived in a squalid caravan.

We'd have to walk past the mobile home park to get to her house, and she'd always ask if she could come over. I'd make up some excuse that I had to go to Asda, anything to stop her discovering the life I was living. The shame of everybody at school knowing was too much to bear.

"So what number do you live at then?" She asked me, "I thought it was just industrial units at the other end of the road, oh and a mobile home park."

I broke into a cold sweat at those words.

After school, Stacey, and I, would walk down the River Nene. We'd creep in behind Matalan and walk down the South bank. Bernie had a friend who lived on a canal boat there, though I can't recall his name. We'd wave as we passed his floating palace that was permanently moored.

That day, I went to the shop near her house on the way home. She must have followed me back because I heard her shout my name, when I turned, I saw her standing at the mobile home park entrance. The game was up, and my lies had caught up with me.

"Why didn't you tell me that you lived here? She said, "It's nothing to be ashamed of really, my aunty lives around here too."

174

She must have been able to tell the shame in my face, however hard I tried to act unfazed. Then she asked to see the caravan I lived in. I felt so ashamed, but the situation couldn't have gotten much worse so I took her and showed her around.

"I can see why you were embarrassed now," she joked. "It's a bit of a shit hole isn't it? But it's your own place and that's cool. Do you live here with anybody else?"

"A friend," I said.

"A man friend?"

I nodded.

"A boyfriend then?"

"No, just a friend."

"Ah, so it's just about the sex then?" she giggled. I shuddered inside. "So when will I get to meet him? Will he be back anytime soon?"

"No," I said, "I've got to meet him in town because we need to go to Asda, he doesn't like people being here when he gets in from work - he's always tired."

"You're always at bloody Asda," she laughed. "I'm having a party next Friday if you want to bring him along? We can all meet him them."

I was relieved to have a way out of this one.

"I can't do Fridays because we go over to Leicester to run the kickboxing class."

"Never mind, I'm sure there'll be other times then."

I walked with her to her house. I didn't really need to go to Asda, I just wanted her out of the way before Bernie came home. He was about ten minutes away.

I ducked past the wall in front of Stacey's house and ran down the road back to the caravan.

She remained my friend afterwards, despite seeing where I was living, she didn't mention it to people at school either, for which I was grateful.

We continued to take walks down the river after school but one day that would change.

I remember that day so vividly. Stacey was wearing a black velvet choker with the word 'BITCH' hanging from it in metal, and I was suffering from terrible hay-fever.

"I've got something I need to tell you," she said. "It's something I've been worried about for a little while now, telling people - that is."

"What's that?"

"I'm bi-sexual, Moll," she sad, as she examined my face for a reaction. "There are a few girls in school I'm attracted to: you included."

I almost laughed when she spoke of it in such a flippant manner.

I was sixteen and immature, I'd just made my first friend only to discover she fancied me. I felt incredibly uncomfortable, that our friendship was over.

"I'm not like *that*, you do understand don't you?"

"Why not? Loads of people at our school are bi-sexual. You don't have a problem with it do you?"

"Look, Stacey." I said, "I'm just not really comfortable talking about it at the minute, okay? It's a lot to take in."

I walked away, leaving her standing on the embankment. I was a little shocked and I felt incredibly uncomfortable. She called out after me but I didn't turn around. I wasn't against her lifestyle choice at all, I just wish she hadn't told me that she found me attractive. All my life, everything seemed to revolve around sex. My dad and his lack of boundaries, Bernie, Bernie's dad, and now Stacey.

Sex, to me, was something I began to associate with everything negative. It wasn't gentle and loving, it was there to degrade and hurt.

As I walked home in tears, I thought about what my parents had said. Maybe they were right and I didn't deserve to have friends. Perhaps I did leave a trail of broken hearts wherever I went. I felt bad for Stacey, but I wished she hadn't burdened me with her problems. I was going through enough turmoil myself.

Bernie was already at the caravan when I got back. I knew he'd be angry but I felt so low that I was almost beyond caring.

"Where the hell have you been?" he said, as I walked in, he didn't take his eyes from the computer screen. We'd finally got dial up internet and he was talking to a young boy in the Yahoo chat rooms as he had been doing so for nearly a week.

"I've been with Stacey," I sniffed.

"Is that the one from school? What does she look like?"

"She's blonde, we've fallen out."

"I'm not surprised, you never seem able to keep friends, Moll. Maybe it's because you're a complete bitch to everybody?"

I took off my coat and ignored him.

"So why did you fall out?"

"She came on to me and I didn't like it," I sniffed.

"She's a lesbian then?"

"No, she's bi-sexual."

"And that's a problem for you?" He turned to look at me with his eyebrows raised."

"It isn't a problem, just a bit of a shock that's all."

"I told you you're a bitch, you'd better make up with her. I think it would be cool to have a lesbian around."

"She'd bi-sexual," I repeated. "I'm going to let the dust settle and then I'll try talking to her, she was upset when I left."

"I'm not surprised," he jumped up, "come on, get your coat back on."

"Why? Where are we going?"

"We're going to Stacey's house so you can apologise to her, then you'll invite her round for dinner tomorrow."

"No Bernie, I'm not doing it," I insisted. The horror of Stacey meeting Bernie was too much to bear, this would destroy what was left of my life.

"I don't know where she lives."

"Don't you lie to me you silly cow, you were round at her house not long ago because you went to her seventeenth birthday party. Have I refreshed your memory yet?"

He bundled me into the car and I sat scared and shaking, my stomach turning in cartwheels.

We drove past Stacey's house and I didn't give anything away. Bernie pulled into a petrol station.

"I'm going to fill up now, if you don't remember where she lives, I'll send you door to door," he shouted. My eardrums felt as though they were going to burst. "We'll stay out all bloody night if we have to."

He went inside to pay for his petrol, and I turned icy cold. I saw Stacey, and her mum, come out of the petrol station carrying a pint of milk. It was a cruel, horrid, coincidence.

I fiddled with the sun visor as they walked to their car, desperate not to be spotted.

They walked past and I was relieved. Then a tap came at the window.

"I thought it was you, Moll," said Stacey. "I'm really sorry about earlier, I don't want to lose you as a friend."

"Don't worry about it," I said, distracted as I kept my eye on Bernie at the checkout. "I'll speak to you tomorrow about it okay?"

"Okay, but you're not going to tell anybody about it at school are you?"

"No, don't worry everything's fine."
Why wouldn't she just leave and get back in her mums car? I could see Bernie laughing and joking with the young checkout assistant as he often did. I wanted Stacey to leave before he came back. Why wouldn't she just get into the damn car before it was too late?

"I was wondering if you wanted to do something this week?" she said.
Bernie had taken his receipt and was walking towards the door.

"We could go the cinema or something like that if you want?"
He was weaving through the cars that were parked in front of us. *Shit!* I said under my breath, as I realized the car in front was causing an obstruction.

"So what do you think, Moll? Can we still be friends?"
Bernie had a curious expression on his face as he walked towards us with his stupid bounce.

"Hello, are you one of Moll's friends from school?"

"Yes, I'm Stacey ... you are?"

"I'm Bernie," he said, holding out his hand. She took it, and I noticed her eyes sweep his greying ponytail and gaunt face.
She gave me an odd look which Bernie was oblivious to.

"Would you like to come over for dinner tomorrow evening?" he asked. "Moll, has never introduced me to any of her friends."
He shot me a glare and I feigned a smile.

"Yes, that would be nice, I was just saying to Moll that we should do something this week."

"I think it's a great idea." said Bernie. "Will about half past six be okay for you?"
She nodded her head.

"It will be nice to get to meet you properly. Do you know where we live Stacey?"

"Yes, I've been to your place once already, though Moll never actually invited me over. I just bumped into her one day."

"Okay then, Petal. We'll see you tomorrow."

"See you then, bye, Moll." She waved at me.
I wanted to go home and pack my bags. I didn't want to live through the nightmare that would be tomorrow evening. Stacey, had quite a lot of respect for me, she wasn't likely to after the way she'd see Bernie treating me.

The car in front of us pulled away and Bernie got into the driver's seat. Stacey finally got in her mum's car as we were blocking access to the pumps.

"Thought you didn't know where she lived," he sneered. "Fucking liar."

Bernie didn't say a word to me for the duration of the journey home. He went into the back porch and lit one of his 'special' cigarettes, before slamming the bedroom door behind him.

181

I took my place on the lounge floor, using my coat as a pillow. The smell of the carpet made me retch, and I shuddered to think what might be living in it.

Chapter Eighteen.

The next morning, Bernie was already dressed and being unusually pleasant. He even offered to drop me off at Asda to pick up the dinner for that evening. He would be driving over to Sleaford to see his disgusting friend, James.

I hated James, he was almost as bad as Bernie. One time, we went over to his house and you could see the fleas jumping off his cat. He was obsessed with computers and making them faster. Once, he minimized the screen and I saw that his desktop was a picture of some children dressed in provocative school wear. It sickened me to my stomach.

Bernie dropped me off at Asda, and I bought the items on his approved list of foods. He also wanted me to pick up four bottles of cola. I bought a shake 'n' vac to try and conceal the smell of the rotten carpet, but I'd dispose of the receipt so he wouldn't find out I'd spent extra money. The walk home was horrendous, my arms were fully stretched as the bottles of cola pulled them to the floor.

I wanted a bath when I got back but there was no hot water whatsoever. The caravan was heated by a small coal fire that heated the boiler.
I had no idea how to use it.
I'd watched Bernie make a fire before and I knew there was coal outside in the mouldy shed, so I tried to put one together.

The dust from the previous fire blew around the living room as I pulled out the pan. I'd sprinkled the shake 'n' vac already so it would eventually get hoovered up. Pure logic helped me to get that fire started and before I knew it, the damp, rotten caravan was comfortably warm.

I got myself into the grimy bath and jumped out just as quick. I'd left the tube of shake 'n' vac on the kitchen worktop. If Bernie were to come back and find it, I'd have been in big trouble. I threw on my bathrobe and carried it to the outside wheelie bin. I had to remove the bags on top and make sure it went right to the bottom of the bin so he wouldn't find it. I left everything exactly as I'd found it.

I went back inside and stared at myself in the mirror. I looked as though I'd aged dramatically and my ribcage protruded. I cried at the hideous sight of fading bruises over my body.

I wanted to go home but I couldn't. The landline was in the living room, all I needed to do was ring them and ask them to pick me up. They might have done but they'd undoubtedly say, *'I told you so'* amongst other things. The thought of them gloating made me decide to stay put, to go through the ordeal that evening with Stacey and Bernie.

I took a blanket from the bedroom cupboard and threw it over the back of a chair in the living room. At least I'd have something to cover myself over with that night if Bernie was in one of his moods again.

A knock at the door came about six o'clock and I panicked. Stacey would see the life I'd been living for the past few months, she'd get to know all about Bernie and how old he was. She'd tell everybody at school and life would be unbearable.

Bernie leaped up to answer the door, it was James. Dopey, disgusting James, who'd bought a sleeping bag, a bottle of whisky, and a large bottle of vodka He handed Bernie a white carrier bag that he took through to the bedroom. At least I now knew why I had to carry all that cola home.

"James is staying for dinner tonight, and he's sleeping over too," he said.
I wanted to ask him what was in the carrier bag but I didn't want to make him angry.

"Food smells good," he smiled. "You can't beat beanfeast."
Before I could answer him, there was another knock at the door. Bernie raced to answer it again as I chopped more vegetables.

"Come on in, Petal," I heard him say. It made me shudder when he called her that. Suddenly, I had the strangest feeling that something was very wrong.

I refused to touch a drop of alcohol - I didn't dare. Stacey was merry before dinner was served. I sat on the floor in silence as they ate like barnyard animals. The alcohol was flowing and the three of them appeared to be forming some kind of bond that unnerved me.

I desperately needed to know what was in the plastic bag because I felt they were planning something.

My opportunity came when Bernie began to demonstrate his martial arts moves on James, (presumably in an attempt to impress Stacey).

"Oh Bernie, you're amazing," she said, as I heard James thud to the floor.

I went into the bathroom and ran the taps, closing the door so he'd think I was in there. Then I crept into the bedroom whilst I could hear their stifled laughs in the living room.

I was right to suspect they'd been planning something.

Inside the bag were two adult schoolgirl costumes with some crotchless underwear, and at the bottom of the bag was a camcorder.

They'd been trying to get us drunk.

I had to get Stacey out.

My hands were shaking and my head was reeling from the discovery, yet I had to keep myself composed to think of a way to save her. I sat in the bathroom for a few moments and got my head together.

I decided to play along for a short while as things were progressing in the living room.

I had to act normal - fun even, and make those dirty old basards think they had the upper hand.

I poured myself a vodka and coke, I didn't want it, but it was a necessary evil. Stacey was falling about the place and even let James have a dance with her.

"Welcome to the party mardy arse," laughed Bernie.

The sexual innuendo's churned my stomach until the two of them decided they were going into the porch to have one of their special cigarettes.

"This is great." she slurred, as she staggered about. "I'll have to go home soon though, Moll. I'm sure a few more drinks won't hurt first though." When they came back into the room, Stacey told them that she'd soon be leaving.

"You can stay here tonight if you want, Petal?" said Bernie. "Just give your mum a call in a bit and tell her where you are. It'll be like a massive sleepover."

I turned away and rolled my eyes. As I did, I caught sight of James's rusty old tobacco tin and it gave me an idea.

"Okay, I'll give her a ring in a bit."

"Somebody has to help us drink all this, mardy arse over there won't," laughed Bernie, again.

"I'm drinking," I smiled, though inside I was screaming for help but nobody could hear me. "It might help if we can have some of your weed though."

I'd never smoked marijuana before, it never appealed to me but I hoped it would get me a few moments alone with her.

I could see Bernie giving me the evil eye, but before he could protest, James had taken hold of his tin and started to roll two 'spliffs.'

"Come on, Stacey, you've done it before haven't you? I'm sure you told me you have."
She nodded her head but looked unsure. I knew she wouldn't want to lose face in front of everybody else so I played on this.

"You joining us?" I asked Bernie and James, knowing they wouldn't because they'd just been.

"Nah, I don't want another one yet thanks," James said, as he leaned back in his chair. He was repulsive in every sense. He had a mass of orange candy floss textured hair and a bushy ginger beard to finish off the look. He smelled as though he hadn't washed for weeks and his hands were grubby and nicotine stained.

"Can I have the back door key please?" I asked Bernie.
He reached into his pocket and threw it across the room at me. I moved out of the way and it landed on the floor.

"Fucking useless, is there anything you can do? Can't even catch a bloody key," he laughed, and the others joined in.

Stacey followed me through to the back porch and I lit up the spliff. I knew I would have about three minutes in there alone with her because that's about how long it took Bernie to smoke.
I closed and locked the porch door behind us, I'd grabbed the front door key off the kitchen table too.

188

Bernie and James were effectively locked inside the caravan.

"Look Stacey," I said.

"You don't need to say anything, Moll," she interrupted, "I won't tell anybody at school that you live in a caravan with a man old enough to be your granddad or something." She laughed. "They're pretty sound actually."

As I watched her struggle with the smoke, it hit me that she was just a kid, desperate to fit in somewhere. Her bi-sexual admission was likely to be a passing phase, and it broke my heart that I had decided to use it against her.

"The truth, Stacey," I sighed, "is that I just don't like your sort."

"My sort? I'm confused, what do you mean?"

"You know, your sort - dykes. You've come into my home and eaten my food. I didn't even want you here. It was him that invited you - not me. Personally, I think you're disgusting."

She was only around five and a half foot tall, that's probably why they bought her costume in a size extra small.

I watched the tears brim and eventually fall from behind her oversized spectacles and I almost crumpled to the floor.

I watched as the cigarette burned its way down to the filter in my hand and I realised I had to act fast as time was nearly up.

I grabbed her around the neck, not tight enough to hurt her, but certainly enough to scare her a bit. I moved my face close to hers.

189

"I don't want to catch anything from you, so why don't you just get the fuck out of my house!" I sneered. "You know, Bernie doesn't like gays either and when I tell him, you won't be leaving here in one piece so I suggest you fuck off now."
I pushed her towards the back door and she stumbled down the steps.

"Tick-tock, Stacey, I'm going to tell them so you'd better get running."
She looked at me from the bottom step, her tears reflected in the lamplight.

"You know what, Moll?" she snivelled, "I used to think you were okay but it turns out you're just trailer trash."
Her comment cut me deep. She was the only friend I had in Peterborough, the only one who had stuck by me regardless of my shameful circumstances, and now I had to let her go.
Stacey turned and fled in a fit of tears.
I estimated it would take her less than ten minutes to get home to safety.
My heart was broken. I had never been homophobic, but I had to make her believe it for her own safety."
Stacey might have hated me, but I'd have hated myself more if anything would have happened to her.

Minutes later, Bernie tapped on the door, closely followed by James.

"Are you pair still smoking in there? Or are you doing something else?" he giggled. "We'd hate to disturb you."

I locked the porch door and went back inside.

"Where's Stacey?" Bernie asked, "Is she messing about outside?" He walked to the back door and looked out over the park.

"She's gone home because she wasn't feeling too good after all that booze. She asked me to apologise on her behalf, she didn't want you both seeing her in a state."

He looked at James and I knew exactly what they were thinking. I'd foiled their plans and for the first time in a while, my smirk came back.

"Oh," was James's contribution to the conversation.

"You'd better get in here then," he sneered, as he pushed me into the bedroom, "James bought you something today."

I never did go back to school after that day.

Chapter Nineteen.

I'll never forget the day Celine came into my life. I'd been struggling to adjust to life in the big world, constantly surrounded by negative, self-destructive people.

The cheap plastic phone rang out in the living area and I ran through the squalor to answer it. Running through that mobile home was like going backwards in time, it was so disgustingly dated I thought I'd always be stuck in the past.

It was the silence of it, there wasn't a damn sound to be heard. I'd grown up in a house with seven other children and was used to noise, I suppose it was one of the many home comforts I was missing.

Since Bernie had placed an advert for the club in the paper, the phone had been ringing frequently.

"Hello? I'm ringing about your advert in the Telegraph, I was wondering if it would be okay to come along tonight and watch to see if it interests me?" said a bubbly voice on the other end.

"You can, but the instructor prefers if you take part. Everybody is pretty much is a beginner there because it's a new class. We won't make you do anything you don't want to. I promise."

Bernie had told me that under no circumstances were people allowed to just come and sit in the hall while he took a class. He said it distracted him and intimidated the students.

"Okay then, what should I wear?"

I ran her through the short list of things she'd need to bring with her.

"My name's Celine, by the way, and I'll be your entertainment for this evening," she laughed.

"I'm Moll," I said. "I look forward to meeting you later, Celine."

After she had hung up, it was as though the sunshine had come out to light up the darkness. It was something in her voice, something that told me I was really going to like Celine.

I promised myself I wouldn't mess up this time. I'd always had problems sustaining friendships with females. It wasn't that I didn't like them, I just couldn't trust them, which resulted in fickle friendships. I'd put Celine on a pedestal already and I hadn't even met her.

Bernie came home from work and asked if we'd had any responses to the advert, I didn't want to tell him about Celine, I wanted to keep her to myself for as long as I could. I had no idea how long it would be until she too would become tainted by Bernie. It seemed all the women would fall for his bullshit lies. They were outrageous lies too, one of his favourite stories he'd tell to his students in the pub after class, was from his days as a 'biker' during the times of Mod's and Rockers.

According to him, he'd upset some people in a pub in Guyhirn one evening. He was on his own and suddenly the place was filled with 'Mods.' From nowhere, all his friends turned up just as he thought he was going to get a kick-in. The climax of his story would be the part where he unbuckled his belt and swiped it across the faces of three men as he slid it out of his trousers, hitting them with the buckle. This didn't make sense to me because I'm sure most buckles wouldn't have fit through the small loops. Even if by some freak chance it had happened, he wouldn't have taken three grown men out with it.

But his students would hang on his every word.

One of his other stories involved a Chinese gang he was involved with. I won't go too much into detail other than to say that when he left this particular gang, he was threatened with a bullet in the head. Not something one would brag about surely? He stayed in contact with a couple of them and would constantly threaten that he'd 'put out a hit on me' if I ever tried to leave him.

I wondered which story he'd use to pull in Celine, and his new students.

Celine stood in the doorway, as I arranged the old jigsaw shaped mats before the class. The hall we rented in the community centre had a huge beech floor and my job was to set everything up while Bernie charmed his new arrivals.

"Have I come to the right place?" she asked me.

"I hope so," I smiled, "unless you were looking for ballroom dancing - which is next door."

She laughed and I felt a little warm flame ignite inside me.

We were inseparable throughout the whole session, she was ten years older than me but it made no difference at all. We giggled like teenagers and she stuck like glue to my side.

"You're very good at all this kung fu stuff aren't you, Moll?" she said, "I suppose it helps having a dad who's into it as well doesn't it?"

I cringed a little but didn't say anything. I didn't want to ruin my new friendship because she thought I was a freak. I wanted to hold onto it for as long as possible before she found out that Bernie was my fiancé. This would be at the end of the session.

"Who's coming to the pub then?" asked Bernie. "We always go to the pub after class, it gives students time to ask me any questions."

There were a couple of volunteers, and to my delight, Celine came too.

I went to use the toilets of the usual dark public house where nobody besides us ever went to drink, and as I was washing my hands, Celine came bounding in.

"Why didn't you tell me he was your fiancé?" she giggled, "I feel silly now."

"That's okay." I laughed. "I hoped you'd feel silly when you found out."

"So how old are you then, Moll?"

I thought back to the incident with Bernie's family, he hadn't told me to lie about my age at the club but I thought the same rule applied so I told her I was nineteen.

195

"Wow, you're just a baby then really aren't you?" she said. "Never mind though, so long as you're okay, you're old enough to know what you're doing eh?"

I could sense her unease about the situation but it seemed that she too desperately needed a friend. There was nothing I didn't like about Celine. She was funny, quirky, and her eyes were always full of wonder and adventure. She was well educated and the most intelligent person I'd ever met, or would meet. She was my perfect, untainted angel.

The good news for me, was that Celine accepted me the way I was. She wasn't interested in my life with Bernie so long as I was okay, she just wanted to be my best friend.

Chapter Twenty.

The classes took off quickly and most nights there would be at least thirty students present. We were training Monday, Tuesday and Thursdays in Peterborough, and Friday's in Leicester. It unnerved me to travel back to my home town every week not knowing who I'd be bumping into. I had a lot of friends from the old club and we'd always go to the pub after class.

Bernie decided that we needed an additional income and allowed me to set up my own junior kickboxing club. He printed off some posters and before I knew it, the class was full of students. It was all I'd ever dreamed of and now it was happening.
Some of the children were as young as five, and their humorous observations of the world brought many a smile to my face. It wasn't without its problems though.

Bernie would turn up at the end of each class to flirt with the mothers as they came to pick their children up, making them well aware that he was my instructor.
He degraded me on so many occasions and it wasn't long before my young students started to lose respect for me, treating me in the same manner that they'd seen Bernie get away with.
There was even an incident with a fire extinguisher one of them had set off whilst I was momentarily

distracted by a crying child. The hall quickly became flooded, and the people that owned the community centre were not impressed at all.

At seventeen, I was making in excess of £300 a week as I slowly introduced a second class.
I told Bernie that he had to stay away from the hall whilst I was teaching because he was putting the students off. He told me that he would do as he pleased, though he never interfered as much afterwards.

It started with dried peas in the beginning, then onto ball-bearings. Bernie had cut up the only pair of jeans I owned to make a small denim bag to fill with dried peas. Then he'd secure it to a bungee strap and hang it from the doorframe.
He forced me to spend two hours each evening punching the small bag as it bounced about the place. He described it as a moving target. It made my knuckles sore and my hands were always covered with friction burns.
When he filled it with ball bearings, the pain was indescribably excruciating. My knuckled would bleed until I could feel little other than a burning throb.
"This was how I learned," he'd say, "this is how they learn over in China, not the poncey crap you get over here."
The worst move Bernie practiced on me was when he pushed his knuckle into an area I believe to be called the 'Jungular Notch,' pushing right down into

it with force. I'd seen him perform the move before on people at the club and had seen full grown men choking on the floor afterwards.

If I tried to back away to avoid absorbing the force, he'd have me up against the wall. He said the only way to execute the move effectively was to know what it felt like. On occasion, he'd use a pole and strike me in the same area.

He was able to viciously attack me and justify himself because he was apparently teaching me some of his most deadlest moves.

We started to attract more females to the class and Bernie appreciated them much more than I did. I found myself constantly concerned for their safety and paranoid that Bernie would try to corrupt them. Michelle, particularly concerned me. She was twenty five years old and quite vulnerable. She had a history of sleeping rough but had recently sought help and landed herself a job as a care assistant. Bernie would obsess over her and it made me sick when I felt a little jealous. Not because I thought he found her attractive, (which he did), but because I felt he'd soon cast me off and I'd be left to fend for myself in a city I barely knew.

He'd bounce over to her during the classes and use her to demonstrate all of his moves at every opportunity.

Then there was his choice of music.

We'd have the stereo playing during training and when Michelle was there, Bernie would make sure his 'The Beatles' cassette was packed.

During the warm up, the song 'Michelle' would play and you could sense the unease in the room. I believe he was secretly trying to send her a message, to groom her even. I'd seen the pattern before with myself and now she was falling for it. From their quiet conversations in the pub, to their whisperings in the corner of the hall. She probably thought he was her ideal man, that she could win him. I almost felt sorry for her.

"Orange, (a UK mobile phone carrier), have sent me some free gifts to choose from," said Bernie, as he pulled a leaflet from his pocket, placing it on the beer soaked table. "One of the gifts is a trip to France for four people. Anybody fancy it?" He looked at Michelle.

"What does it include?" she asked.

"It includes a return ferry and two nights stay at a campsite in Calais."

"Yeah, I'm up for that," she grinned.

"You'll need to sort yourself a passport out, Moll," said Bernie.

I'd never had a passport, we'd barely taken any family holidays during my childhood so I never had a use for one.

"I'll need to get my birth certificate first," I said.

"You can make a start on that tomorrow then can't you?"

I wasn't supposed to talk to Bernie in the pub after class. He insisted that it was his time to speak to the students and answer any questions. I often found myself sitting on my own in silence with a pint of cider, unless Celine was there of course, she was on holiday though.

It wasn't long before Bernie invited Michelle to join the Friday class in Leicester. She'd come with us in the car, and Bernie would always make me sit in the back because Michelle was older than me. I struggled to hear their conversations sometimes but did notice one occasion where she put her hand on his thigh, I watched his expression in his rear view mirror and it sickened me.
I felt very odd about Michelle coming with us, almost as her being in my hometown tainted it a little.
I hated her coming to the pub with all my old friends afterwards too, I felt as though she'd invaded my life. Her constant flirting with Bernie was getting on my nerves.
The landlady didn't once question my age and would quite happily let me drink pints of cider and order from the bar. Bernie liked the land lady, though he liked her daughter more.
Her name was Polly and she was around my age. She had long blonde hair and Bernie would often refer to her as 'young and innocent' or 'angelic'.

After the pub, we'd make our way over to Barbara's house: Bernie's ex-girlfriend. Apparently some of Bernie's possessions were there. He went every week and I'd sit in the car on her driveway for rarely less than an hour.

When Michelle brought the subject up one night on the driveway, she asked me if it bothered me that Bernie spent so much time with his ex still. I told her that I was used to it because it happened every week. I had complained about it before, but he told me I was being a selfish cow. Barbara apparently had nobody else apart from Lou, and she was lonely.

I sent off for my birth certificate, Bernie had written a cheque to the registry office and I'd filled out the form myself. I assumed my place of birth would be the same as my siblings, who were all born in the Leicester Royal Infirmary. An envelope came back soon afterwards which would confirm I was wrong. Bernie was angry because they'd cashed the cheque too.

"I want you to ring them and get my money back," he yelled. "I will not have you ruining our holiday plans."

There was no point in me doing this, you pay for the search as well as the certificate, it said so in their small print.

"Our holiday plans?" I spat. "More like *yours and Michelle's* holiday plans, I know what's going on, don't think I'm stupid, Bernie."

"You stupid bitch," he shouted, and smacked me across the face. My cheek was burning and I wanted to cry.

"I've had enough of your shit, you're just a jealous little cunt." He threw me against the window and swiped at my face again.

"And you're just a fucking pervert!" I screamed.

It didn't hurt until I saw the blood pooling from underneath my top. Bernie had attacked me with a screwdriver. It had been left on the side from the previous evening when he'd tried to fiddle the electric coin meter.
I didn't know how deep the wound was, he'd plunged forwards but my natural instincts had me turning off at an angle to deflect some of the blow. Perhaps it had only grazed the skin.
I felt light headed and fell against the rickety kitchen table. I think I must have fainted because when I woke up, Bernie was at the side of me and he'd dressed my wound. He'd left me uncovered from the waist up.

"Look, Moll, I'm sorry for what happened but you really made me angry. You know I'm not interested in Michelle, she's a fucking tramp and her sister is a junkie. You can't go making accusations like that. When you called me a pervert, I just flipped. You know I'm not a pervert, I can't understand why you'd say such a thing."
I didn't dare move a muscle, I was in a very vulnerable position so I just nodded and went along with whatever crap Bernie threw at me about hurting his feelings. Then I apologized.

I had to take a couple of days off from training because I didn't want to disturb my wound. This meant that Bernie had to take over my junior class for me which I hated. He'd always comment how the girls were like little angels and incredibly supple and flexible for their ages. He made me sick.

He constantly pestered me about my birth certificate, asking me to ring my parents and find out where I was born. I refused to do it and the holiday was off. I didn't care one little bit, I was glad I'd scuppered Bernie and Michelle's romantic getaway whilst I tagged along.

"Looks like the holiday is off," I heard Bernie say to Michelle on the phone. "Moll can't get her shit together to sort out her passport. Sorry about that, Pet, I know you were looking forward to it."
I was pleased with this result

On Friday we were in the pub after training, I sipped on my Strongbow in a corner when my brother, Alex, walked in. I wanted to duck under the table but I was frozen to the spot. He gave Bernie an evil look and came to sit next to me.

"How are you, sis?" he asked, as he gave me a hug, quite out of character. "Everybody is missing you at home."

"Are they?" I asked, trying to disguise the lump in my throat. I wanted to tell Alex about Bernie, how he'd been mistreating me, how he'd stabbed me with a screwdriver, and how I desperately wanted to go back but didn't think I'd be welcome. He leaned over and sang part of a Westlife song in my ear.

"How does that sound?" he asked, "Does it sound okay? Me and my friends are performing here tonight and I don't want to make an idiot of myself."

He explained how he was now part of a boy band. I looked around the room, it was normally quite deserted in there, however, this evening there were considerably more people than usual. Mainly flushed middle aged women.

Then his friends arrived and they took to their microphones to sing cover songs. The place filled up very quickly and soon it was packed wall to wall with screaming women, the band wasn't half bad.

"That's my brother," I said proudly to the students from the club. We fought our way to the bar and my brother winked at me during one of his solos.

I looked towards the corner of the room through the thin mist of dry ice that came from the smoke machine. It changed colour from the disco lights and through it, I could see Bernie sat on his own. He glared at me but I wasn't afraid of him this time, my family apparently missed me which gave me a glimmer of hope and the upper hand over Bernie.

Alex disappeared before I had the chance to say goodbye properly. I had so many questions to ask but he waved awkwardly to me whilst a lady, (dressed way younger than her actual age), tried to pull the shirt from his back.

"So what did Alex have to say for himself then?" scoffed Bernie, as we drove back to Peterborough. "I notice he completely ignored me, how rude, especially after all the quality training I gave him.

He's turned into a real big head, Moll." He stuck his nose in the air.

"He said they all missed me."

"I bet he did, they're poisoning him against us Moll, can't you see it? You're lucky you got out when you did. It'll just be another game, I'm sorry to tell you this but they don't give a fuck about you. You could get hit by a bus tomorrow and I'd be the only person at your funeral. I'm the only one who cares about you. I'm the one who put a roof over your head when you had nowhere to go."

I just wanted to tell him to shut his fat fucking mouth, I couldn't understand why I wanted to defend my family after the way they'd treated me in the past. Maybe they'd learned from their mistakes? I was certainly learning from mine.

I said nothing in response but inside I was smiling.

Chapter Twenty One.

As Friday soon came around again, I'd done little other than think about seeing Alex in the pub again. I'd hoped he'd visit and answer my questions.

I'd been toying with the idea of going home all week; fantasizing how I'd just pack my things and tell Bernie to stick his squalid caravan up his arse and never having to look at his ugly face again. My parents would welcome me with open arms and the past would be erased.

Bernie's sister, Anne, wanted to come to Leicester with us to see what her little brother Bernie had achieved. She had a long history of drug abuse but was incredibly pleasant to me. We shared a mutual hate for hers and Bernie's father. Unfortunately, she was almost always half cut and crazy.

I could cope with her coming along to the class, she was of no threat to me and she always made fun of Bernie which made me smile.

At the end of the class, he took a call on his new mobile phone, it was one of his friends from Leicester.

"Yes of course, Mike, we'd love to. See you soon."

"Who was that?" I asked.

"Mind your own business you nosey cow," he snapped.

"Don't talk to her like that you jumped up little prick," said Anne. "Who do you think you are?" She put her arm around me and Bernie glared. In any other situation, I might have felt protected, but Anne was Bernie's sister. The smell of her body odour and lasts nights alcohol seeped from her pores and turned my stomach.

"Whose coming pub then?" asked one of the students in a way that Bernie would normally ask.

"Not tonight I'm afraid," said Bernie. "You'll have to go on without us, we've got somewhere to be."

My heart sank to the bottom of my stomach.

"But why not?" I asked.

What about Alex? What if he was to come looking for me and assumed I didn't hang out there anymore?

"Mind your own," he replied.

I walked into the toilets and sobbed gently. I remembered those toilets from years ago when I attended St. Johns Ambulance. The toilet paper was a dull pink back then. I wanted to go back to the times of the pink toilet paper, a time before Bernie. I could hear him talking to Anne in the hallway.

"They're really nice people once you get to know them Anne. You'll be fine as long as you don't show me up. They've got free beer too..."

This was the deal-maker for her, she was an alcoholic and Bernie knew it.

I quickly realised that my night in the pub had been sacrificed for a house party with Bernie's drug taking friends. The friends with the filthy matted dreadlocks, the friends who smelled so bad because they likely hadn't changed their underwear for weeks. They were the ones who rode manically around the town on their quad bikes and trikes, high on whatever was flavour of the week.

I crept out of the toilets and stood behind Bernie, waiting for him to finish his conversation with Anne.

"Can't I just go to the pub and you pick me up from there in a bit?" I asked.

He smirked at me and screwed up his nose.

"No, you can't just go to the pub and have me pick you up later. Anne doesn't know anybody around here, I need you to keep an eye on her."

"But I don't want to go to Mike's house," I whined, "I want to go to the pub instead."

"And I want you to stop being a stupid bitch but it won't happen will it?"

He pushed past me and said farewell to his students, I watched enviously with a heavy heart as they left the building to walk into town together.

The three of us were left to lock up and suddenly I began to hate my life again.

The house party was in full swing by the time we arrived. It was a medium sized council house with an overgrown garden. The smell of dog shit hit me as I walked up the path.

'It'll only be for an hour or so, two at the most and I can live with that because it will end eventually'. I told myself.

The music was incredibly loud and echoed around the street, the neighbours knew better than to complain though.

We'd been there less than half an hour and the caring Anne had turned into nasty, drunken Anne who fell about the place and made a show of herself. I had no idea how much she'd drank but I feared the night wouldn't end well.
 The house was in a squalid state with people being sick on the floor and urinating freely.

Bernie ignored me and sat in the living room smoking weed, and talked about how spiritually enlightened he was. People listened to him over the music as they drank and injected themselves with drugs I knew nothing about.
I'd drank a fair bit myself to wash away the pain of not seeing my brother that evening, the more I drank, the further away the memory became, almost like that little blip on the television screen after you turn it off.
I staggered upstairs to find Anne. People were laying half conscious on the landing, slumped up against the wall with saliva gathering on their chins like rabid dogs.
I slumped on the top step and held my head in my hands. Anne emerged from one of the bedrooms and flopped beside me.

"What's up, chicken?" she asked, as she put one of her huge smelly arms around me. I could feel her sweat against my skin.

"I was supposed to meet my brother at the pub tonight but Bernie wouldn't let me go." I confessed, knowing too well that she'd have no recollection of the conversation in the morning.

"You've got all the family you need here, chicken. I know what'll cheer you up, come and have a dance."

"No, I'm okay thanks, I've got a headache. I'll just sit here for a bit."

"I'll be back in a minute, Moll, you just wait here."

She patted me on the arm and disappeared back into the bedroom. The sound of jungle music and manic laughter filled the whole of the upstairs.

'Welcome to hell, Moll.' I said underneath my breath.

One of the half-conscious girls opened her eyes and looked at me.

"I want my mum," she slurred, as her eyes slowly closed again. I was terrified.

"I've got something for your headache," said Anne, as she leaned over me.

She gave me a white tablet and I had no reason to suspect she'd given me anything other than a paracetamol. It looked rather like one.

After a short while, I began to load my body with shots of vodka. I was being sick anywhere there was a surface and I didn't care. I was completely uninhibited.

I jumped up and down on the beds upstairs as the music repeated over and over in my head. I was practically bouncing off the walls. Everybody thought it was hilarious. I assumed they were laughing with me.

I found myself downstairs in the kitchen, searching for more alcohol. As I tried to take the cap off a bottle of beer, I realised that my hands wouldn't function. It was the strangest thing.

My mind was sharp and crystal clear, I was well aware of the things going on around me and the conversations people were having, I just couldn't control my body.

I'd been drinking for hours and I still felt perfectly sober.

I wanted to find Anne to explain how I was feeling but my legs wouldn't hold me up as I got to the foot of the stairs. I had to crawl.

'What the hell am I doing?' I thought to myself, as I fell against the stairs. *'What the hell is wrong with me? Am I dying?'*

I put my hands out in front of me and dug my nails into the piss soaked carpet, my legs were trailing behind. It was mainly a job for my arms to pull my weight up to the next few steps. I could feel the urine contaminating the area beneath my fingernails as they picked up all the damp dirt on the way.

I looked through the shit smeared slatted banister and heard a dog yelping as it was held down and kicked repeatedly in the head by Bernie's 'lovely' friends.

I'd returned to the top step again and the semi-conscious girl was being carried into a room by somebody I didn't recognize. I couldn't move, there was nothing I could do to stop it.

I cradled my head in my hands again and begged for the music to stop. My brain felt as though it was convulsing each time the music kicked in.
I lost complete control of my bladder but I was more concerned about my heart that was kicking from inside my chest as if to say: *'What have you done to me?'*

Through the confusion, I heard Bernie's voice yelling at Anne.

"What the hell have you given her? She's fucking paralytic."

"I gave her a Dexy's, Bernie, she was being a right miserable, stuck up cow and I didn't like it, okay?"

"Look at her!" he shouted. "She's underage, sheshouldn't be drinking or taking drugs; they could kill her. She's only seventeen"

"For god sake lighten up, I only gave her one. She'll be coming down from it soon."
I had faith in my body, as alien as it felt to me, I trusted it not to give up on me.

"Get your coat, Anne. I'm taking you both back."
I thought I'd tried to stand up, but I must have rocked forwards instead because I crashed down the stairs. My body just went with the fall like a piece of putty. I think this was the reason I didn't sustain

any injuries besides a couple of bruises. It jolted me into consciousness though.

"Moll, darling, are you okay? You've just fallen down the stairs." Mike's haggard wife came to my assistance with a cigarette hanging from her poisonous gob.

"I'm seventeen," I smiled. "Just seventeen." Bernie scooped me up in his arms and carried me out the front door.

"This makes you some kind of paedo then doesn't it, Bernie?" shouted one of his friends from the doorway. "You fucking nonce!"

"Fuck off," he retaliated, as he bundled me into the car. "Get in the fucking car Anne before they come out and kick your head in."

"It's your fault for saying she was seventeen Bernie, going on what you first told everyone, she should be twenty now."

"Give it a rest will you, Anne, you're getting on my nerves now. If you don't shut up then you'll be walking back okay?"

We drove to a nearby petrol station and Bernie got me a bottle of water and a coffee.

"You've got to sober up, Moll, the whole town is swarming with police tonight. If we get pulled over and they see the state you're in, you'll get locked up for taking drugs. Can't you see how serious this is?" I didn't say much but I spat the hot coffee out all over the disgusting, walnut trimmed dashboard.

"Sober up, Moll!"

"Fuck off dipshit!" I yelled at him.

"Don't talk to my brother like that you fucking whore, who the fuck do you think you are?"
Anne reached her led across and kicked the back of my chair, spilling the scalding coffee over my legs.

"You're a fucking liability, Moll," said Bernie, and he made his way towards the A47.

"I need a piss," said Anne. "Stop the car."

"I'm not stopping until we're back in Peterborough," said Bernie, "You'll have to wait, in case you didn't notice, we passed a police car back there."

"If you don't pull over then I'll piss on the seat you wanker," her voice was deafening and she kicked the back of Bernie's seat. She had turned into a crazed animal.

"Fuck off you crazy bitch, I'll give you a smack in the mouth if you don't quit it."
Anne unfastened her seatbelt and opened the rear passenger door. The breeze chilled me to the bone as it circulated the car. The sound of the open road scared the shit out of me as I thought she was going to jump out.

"Get that fucking door shut now!" yelled Bernie.

"No, I won't." she sobbed, and opened it as far as it would go. She stretched out her leg to keep it open as Bernie desperately tried to reach into the back and grab the handle.

I caught a glimpse of my reflection in the vanity mirror; red and blue lights lit up my face, closely followed by the wailing sirens.

"Anne," he said desperately, "If you've got any pills, then throw them in the foot well now. Anne, are you fucking listening to me?"

Through her hysterical tears, she pulled a bag from her pocket. It was full of the tablets she'd given me at the house.

"Moll, I need you to reach into the back without looking obvious, and pick them up."

I sunk low into my seat and grabbed at the bag on the floor, slowly bringing my arm back into the front.

"Now I need you to take this," he pulled out a small, sealed bag with a lump of cannabis inside. "Put it down your top. They won't check you because you're so young."

I didn't think anything of it and stuffed the drugs into my bra.

Bernie pulled over in a layby and got out to greet the officers. The back door was still wide open and I listened as he spoke about Anne.

He told them that she suffered from a mental illness and had drank a little too much that evening, that he was taking her home to rest.

They breathalysed him, as he hadn't been drinking that evening, the results were negative.

I composed myself as an officer walked around the car until he was standing right next to my window. He shone his torch on the tax disc and briefly on me but that was all.

Anne received a warning from them and we continued the journey home in silence.

"You stupid bitch, Anne," said Bernie, "you almost got us all in trouble. I suggest you sort your fucking life out or you get out of mine."
We dropped her off outside her grotty flat, and I never saw her again after that.

Chapter Twenty Two.

We managed to get away on holiday eventually. It wouldn't be France, but I'd been put off that idea anyway. Michelle had left the club after me and her went on a night out. We were both quite drunk and we ended up scrapping. I got thrown out of the nightclub, and she lost two teeth. She was eight years older than me so I decided she got what she deserved. I saw nothing of her after that.

I started to spend much more time with Celine, she made me laugh until my stomach ached, all the good she did almost outweighed the bad that was happening. Celine made me stronger. At twebty eight, she lived at home with her parents.

We'd go shopping together and I'd meet her by the big clock that stood inside the Queensgate Centre opposite New Look. Bernie constantly refused me money so I didn't have a penny to spend on our shopping trips, unlike Celine. We had a lot of laughs regardless.
She unknowingly provided the normality I so desperately craved.

It was a relief to get out of the caravan, and Celine's eyes would always light up when she saw me approaching the clock. You could pick her out of a crowd easily with her enormous smile and silly hats.

We headed to the department store where we sprayed each other with the worse smelling perfumes we could find. She'd bought a pair of tickets for a fashion show and begged me to go along with her. I knew nothing about fashion but I went along for the company. When we were there we danced like lunatics to 'Absolutely Everybody' by Vanessa Amorosi, as the models walked up and down the catwalk. People were too busy pointing and laughing at us, than paying any attention to the atrocities on stage in front of us.

After that, we headed to her favourite shop: Monsoon.

She picked out a pink mandarin style dress which she tried on. She loved the dress so much, that she swore she'd get married in it one day.

We walked through the lingerie section afterwards and used the larger sized bras to catapult things at each other from opposite sides of the shop.

Afterwards, we went back to her parents' house and danced around the living room to 'Music' by Madonna. Whenever she used to greet me, she'd say: 'Hey Mr. DJ' because she loved the song. I became DJ Moll. Then she climbed on her parents' coffee table and danced to 'Silence' by Delerium. It was her favourite song. Her parents were in bed so most of our laughter was of the silent tear-streaming variety. She had a shirtless photo of Jackie Chan as her desktop wallpaper and I teased her about it. She put on a song by Air called 'Sexy Boy' and we giggled about it.

She opened an email on her computer.

"Look, I've met this really nice bloke online. His name is Robbie"

"Where is he?" I asked her, "you have to be careful talking to people online, you don't know who's on the other side of the computer."

"He's in Brisbane, don't worry, he isn't a weirdo, we've been talking for months now. I'm saving up for a ticket to go over and meet him." She looked excited as her crescent shaped eyes lit up with adventure.

I smiled for her, but on the inside I was concerned that she was going to travel to the other side of the world to meet someone she didn't know. On a more personal, selfish level: I didn't want my best friend to leave me.

"It won't be happening for a long time yet though," she reassured me. "It's going to take me ages to save up for a return ticket."

I breathed a sigh of relief, I had time to convince her otherwise.

Celine would come to the Leicester class with us on Fridays, I loved having her there and everybody liked her. Even though she was pleasant to Bernie, she didn't hang on his every word like the others did. It almost seemed as though she was just there to be my friend.

After the pub, she'd sit in the car with me whilst Bernie paid his weekly visit to Barbara for an hour. She never mentioned the odd situation and we just talked the time away.

I employed her as an assistant instructor for my junior kickboxing class. Being fairly new, she wasn't able to teach but she would help me to keep an eye on them to avoid any fire extinguisher incidents happening. The children loved Celine and the feeling was mutual, she was fantastic with them. I finally felt as though life was giving me a little something back, that I'd been through so much grief to get to where I was. My only problem now was Bernie, but even he had been leaving me to get on with things. It was as though Celine had somehow made me stronger.

We took a holiday to Lyndhurst in The New Forest. Bernie, had been accepted as an Instructor into a well known kung fu association, and I'd been offered the opportunity to be accepted onto the National Wushu squad. It would mean travelling all over the world if I'd be accepted and it was something Bernie had always wanted for himself (except he was too old).

The association's headquarters were in Southampton so we camped nearby. Celine came with us, as did George,(a young student of Bernie's from Peterborough). He was fourteen years old and had studied Taekwondo for a couple of years. He really looked up to Bernie and idolised him. Celine, and I, went for a walk around the new forest whilst Bernie and George went over the syllabus as George was preparing for his next grading.

The forest was almost magical as we watched the ponies wandering about freely. I couldn't get over how much space there was amongst the trees.
We found an old bicycle and it became our mode of transport. I would croggy Celine about on it and we'd use it to take trips to the local shop. It was funny because the thing was falling apart.

"You're acting like a fucking kid, will you stop it?" said Bernie, as he pulled me to one side.

"I am a fucking kid," I reminded him.
He turned all his attention to George, taking him through the green belt syllabus.

That night, Bernie rolled himself a spliff. George was a little shocked when he saw him do it, he was from a well to do family and he really idolised Bernie.
Celine, and I, shared a spliff for fun. Celine was from a very respectable family but she sometimes liked to let her hair down. She coughed continuously before deciding that it wasn't for her.

"At least I can say I've tried it," she giggled.
George wanted to try some but Bernie wouldn't let him smoke. Instead, he took some of the resin and crumbled it into a pan of milk he was warming on the camping stove. He gave it to George to drink.
Me and Celine lay on the car bonnet and looked up at the stars. I pointed out the constellations to her. She was quite into astrology, though I'd never really given it much thought apart from noticing that all my closest friends in the past, (including Celine); were Aquarius's. George fell asleep by the

campfire and Bernie shouted me into the tent. I told him I had to make sure George made it into bed okay because he was passed out by the fire, but Bernie was having none of it. It hated him because of it, George was only fourteen years old, he'd given him drugs, and left him to sleep under the stars. It just wasn't acceptable.

He attacked me again that night. I tried to be silent through my muffles as he held his hand over my face. I didn't want anybody to hear the shame of what I regularly went through.
I couldn't sleep, my whole body hurt and felt dirty as I crawled out of the tent to take a walk to the shower block. It was starting to get light and George was still passed out in front of where the fire had been burning. Celine had made it back to the tent I'd guessed. I knew the spliff had affected her also. George almost looked dead as he lay on the grass. His skin was pale and the morning frost began to settle upon his clothing. I gave him a nudge just to make sure he was okay.

"George, wake up. You fell asleep outside last night. Get yourself into your sleeping bag otherwise you're going to get sick and catch your death out here."
He grunted to acknowledge me, and he crawled into his tent.

After I'd showered, Celine was waiting outside for me.

"There's something I want to tell you, Moll," she said.

My heart sank, the last time somebody wanted to tell me something, it was Stacey, and that didn't end well at all.

We walked back to our tents and Celine tried to communicate the best she could.

"When I was at school, I was molested by my P.E. teacher. I couldn't say anything to anybody because I was so scared at the time. Looking back as an adult, I wish I'd just told somebody and reported it, stop him doing it to somebody else. Do you know what I mean?"

I could see exactly the point she was trying to make, she had heard what Bernie had done the night before.

I tried to shrug it off and ignore the comment before my face burned with shame.

"At least you got away in the end, Celine," I said, and I patted her affectionately on the shoulder. My situation was more complicated than that, I had no way out, nowhere to go and nobody to turn to that could help me.

Bernie was awake when we got back to the camp, he behaved like nothing had happened. He and George, (who now had a sore throat from the cold and had almost lost his voice), decided to go into Southampton to train at the headquarters. I was unable to go because my body felt sore and I was consumed by the usual sickness that normally came after Bernie's attacks. It looked as though I would miss the opportunity to try out for the Wushu squad. I no longer wanted to be a part of Bernie's dream.

Celine didn't go to the training centre either, she came with me instead and we visited the Southampton docks. We watched the boats for a while ,talked about boys and anything else that came into our minds. When I needed to be silent, Celine would stand in silence with me also. I wanted to be on one of those boats so desperately, drifting out to sea, never to be found again. Celine could come with me of course. But Bernie would get thrown overboard if he thought he'd be coming too.

Chapter Twenty Three.

I became quite well known for teaching around Peterborough, and a short while after I was offered a paid opportunity to develop a twelve week self-defence course for a local school to add to their curriculum.

They would be paying me £50 a session and pay any travelling expenses. It was quite an achievement considering the students I was teaching were only a couple of years younger than me. Then another opportunity came when I was asked to teach ladies self-defence on a Sunday at the local mosque. I didn't realise how much of an honour it was to have been asked. I was completely ignorant to their culture, and on the first day, I walked through the doors with my arms revealed. A young white female wearing a spaghetti strapped top.

Celine, had almost saved up enough money for that return ticket to Australia, and every day I worried about being left behind on my own. I wasn't sure I could stay strong without having Celine to call on when I needed her.

Another surprise visit came in the form of Beryl; she came into the pub one Friday after class. I'd seen my brother on and off over the months, though he didn't often speak of my family missing me anymore, it was more his disappointment for me not coming home after I suppose he's told them he'd managed to change my mind. I suppose he wanted to be a hero in my parent's eyes. It was too difficult for me to let him have that title though. They didn't understand how difficult it was for me to leave. To return home to uncertainty, to the abusive, paranoid ways of my father, and my mum's emotional vacancy.

"Happy birthday, Moll. I can't believe you're legally old enough to drink now," said Beryl, her niceties were unnatural, she was clearly choking on the words as she forced them out.

"Everyone has bought you a present for your birthday," she said, as she handed me a cardboard bag filled with gifts. I was moved by the gesture, but I still thought it was a trick to get me to go home.

"Mum, and Dad, told me to ask if you wanted to go and visit them sometime. They said they understand you live over in Peterborough now, but they'd like to see you anyway."
A no strings attached visit? I wanted to say yes but I couldn't commit. Bernie wouldn't allow it anyway. He hated my family and wouldn't even acknowledge my sister.

I walked her back over to the car park as one of the students left at the same time.

"Good luck for next week, Moll. Don't get cold feet will you?"

"What's happening next week?" said Beryl. "Are you getting bloody married to that paedo? You're not are you?"

"No, I've got a competition next week, that's all."

"Okay, well look after yourself then. I'll tell Mum and Dad that you'll think about it okay?"

"I can't promise anything," I said. I didn't want her giving them the wrong message.

"Why don't you just stop putting them through all this heartbreak and go see them?" she said, from the safety of her car.

"See you later Beryl," I said, and I walked back towards the pub.

I could have gone home if I'd wanted to. My parent's house was about fifteen minutes walk from where I was. I could have vanished and Bernie would never have seen me again. My heart told me to go home but my mind told me I still wouldn't be safe. I was trapped and preyed upon wherever I went. At least I had a little control over my life at the moment.

There was no impending competition, Bernie had booked the registry office for the fourth of November 2000. They said I'd have to wait a week after my birthday before I could get married because they had to put a public notice out.

He had also hired the Community Centre in Peterborough that we trained at for the wedding reception. I was dreading it, and I didn't get a say in anything. *It's only a piece of paper,* I told myself, *I can always get divorced when I do eventually leave him.* It was inevitable, or perhaps it wasn't. I'd fantasized about it continually, it was the fantasies, and Celine that were pulling me through.

My wedding dress would be borrowed from Jeff's wife. Jeff, was an old friend of Bernie and had trained at the Leicester club for years before I'd started. He'd served in the army and he'd also be the person giving me away at the wedding. Not because I liked him, because I didn't. I thought he was creepy. It was Bernie's decision.

The only silver lining was that Celine would be there and I was allowed to have her as my bridesmaid. So long as she was there I would be able to get through anything.

Unfortunately, I couldn't afford to buy her a dress so she said that she'd sort one herself.

Back in the pub, Bernie, had left my bag of gifts unattended and the students had all left. Bernie was stood at the bar chatting up Polly, who looked desperate to escape. I went and sat back at the table only to find that he'd already unwrapped my presents.

"Told you they didn't give a fuck," he said, as he swaggered over. "It's your eighteenth birthday and they bought you a load of old shit, there's nothing of any value in there."

Bernie hadn't bought me anything for my birthday but I didn't mention it. I didn't really care.

To me, it wasn't about how much they spent, it was the fact that they'd remembered. I looked through the bag: there was a pair of shoes and a jumper. I'd been wearing the same pair of shoes for the past two years and they barely kept my feet dry anymore.

I dug a little deeper into the bag and found a box of coloured fairy lights. They'd remembered how I'd enjoyed decorating my bedroom with strange items when I lived with them. There was also an inflatable 'Mr. Happy' from the Mr. Men. He was about a metre tall. I knew exactly where I'd put him once I'd get back to the caravan and blown him up. I thought he was great.

There was no visit to Barbara's house that evening, the last time he visited she had pushed him out the door telling him to 'fuck off' and never return. He'd taken her some flowers because they were still 'friends' and she was a lonely old woman according to Bernie.

Bernie, fiddled with the key and pulled at an envelope that stuck out from underneath the door mat. The caravan didn't have a letter-box so somebody had left a birthday card under the mat. He took it inside and opened it.

As it was a birthday card, I assumed it for me. He opened the card carefully and tipped the contents into the envelope, then he threw the card in the bin.

"Who was that from?" I asked.

"It was from Cumbrian, Tom."

I remembered Cumbrian Tom, I hated him. He had some land in the Lake District and we visited him once. He lived as a hermit halfway up a mountain in a derelict house. Apparently, he used to be quite well off but his wife had left him and taken most everything he owned. He was left with this derelict property and clung to the hope that one day it would be fit for him to live in. He resided in a caravan just outside it. Bernie, and I, had taken a tent.

The house had no windows or doors, it had no mains electricity and at night it was pitch black upon that mountain. It was terrifying to hear the wind whistling through the empty spaces of the building where the windows once sat.

I had to catch food for dinner one evening, Tom, and Bernie, had sent me down to the river to catch a fish. When I came back with nothing, it turned out they had been to Tesco and bought food for that night anyway. They thought it was hilarious and I hated them all the more for it. I'd got lost down by the river, if I hadn't found my way back before darkness it's likely I wouldn't have come back. They completely underestimated how appalling my eyesight was.

"So what's in the envelope then?" I asked him.
"Mushrooms. My birthday present to you."
"Mushrooms?"
"Yes, you know, the magical sort."

Bernie, had been saying for a long time that he wanted to get some mushrooms, that he had taken them back in the day, and how much fun they were. I'd just gone along with it and nodded. I never expected he would actually get some for me. I was horrified at the idea of taking drugs, even though they were natural and had been picked from the Lake District. Tom, said it was something to do with sheep urination, that's what caused the hallucinogenic effect according to him.

I could not have foreseen spending the remainder of my birthday taking a hallucinogenic. I wanted to protest but Bernie would have called me ungrateful and probably laid into me anyway, saying that I'd thrown his gesture back in his face.

He'd taken the liberty of putting up the fairy lights in the living room and inflating *my* Mr. Happy. It made me feel sick that he'd inflated Mr. Happy, so long as I had it, it would always have Bernie's germs on it somewhere near the mouthpiece.

He fixed the lights to the wall around the alcove and Mr. Happy stood inside.

"If you don't want the mushrooms, Moll, you can fuck off and find somewhere else tonight. I'm not having my experience ruined by you."

He flicked on the TV/DVD combo and put on his Father Ted DVD. He sat on a patio chair and I sat on the floor. Bernie divided the mushrooms in half.

"You can either eat them or smoke them he said. What do you want to do?"

I didn't know anything about drugs, I'd been spiked once by his sister, Anne, but I was doing it of my own free will this time.

"Don't I need to cook them to eat them?" I asked him.

"You're a stupid bitch, Mol," he said, and he threw half into his mouth and swallowed them. So I copied him and returned to my seat on the floor with my back against the wall.

I wasn't sure whether or not I'd dozed off, but suddenly I was hyperconscious. I became acutely

232

aware of my body as it sank into the floor, beneath the veil of fog that lay thick just above the carpet. I tried to ignore it and focus on Father Ted.

I could see the twinkling fairy lights from the corner of the room, they seemed much brighter and warmer now. I could almost feel the heat radiating from them.Though the lights weren't the chasing variety, they appeared to dance, to reach out their colourful rays and touch me. The red ones were hot though and I remember flinching from them.

I concentrated once more on Father Ted, then something from the corner of my eye caught my attention again. It was Mr. Happy, lurking sinisterly in the corner, *'he'd probably become contaminated by Bernie's saliva,'* I thought, and it terrified me.

I tried not to look at him again but each time I turned towards the TV, I would see him in my peripheral vision, moving just that little bit closer. My eyes would flick back to the TV and he'd appear larger and closer than before. Every time I looked over to the corner of the room, Mr. Happy would be perched where he'd been placed, like butter wouldn't melt.

I turned back to Father Ted and he was right up against the side of my face, his head was huge and his eyes were no longer playful slits of black plastic. His mouth was host to a line of razor sharp teeth that were dripping with black slime.

I jumped out of my skin almost and looked back over to the corner. Mr. Happy was back in his spot again. I wanted it to end, so I got myself up and

took him from the side. I stuffed him into a cupboard and went to bed.
I decided I'd never touch anything like that again, I could see how it messed people up.

The next day, Celine, wanted me to go over to her house to discuss bridesmaid dresses with her. She'd struggled to decide which colour would best match the monstrosity I was borrowing.

"I think the champagne colour would go quite well, what do you think?" she asked me. I was still shocked from the previous evening and was probably quieter than usual.

"Whatever you think, Celine, I'm really not fussy which colour you choose. Just pick something you like and we'll go with that."

"Don't you want to get married?" she asked, as she slumped in the chair next to me. "Your heart doesn't seem to be in it. If you're not sure about it then you should call the whole thing off."
I imagined it for a moment; me calling the whole thing off, Bernie's face as I jilted him at the registry office. I could even turn up pissed and shout profanities at him, the people at the registry office would call the police and they'd ask me about Bernie - I'd tell them everything. Then I'd be free from him and he'd be taken in for questioning.
I decided to make the day about Celine instead.

"Don't be daft," I said, "if you like this dress, then let's go in into town and find it so you can try it on."

The morning of the wedding quickly arrived and Bernie went off to meet the students who had travelled up from Leicester for the event. They were staying in a hotel around the corner. Jeff, was bringing the wedding dress over with him and I couldn't have it until just before the wedding when he'd come to pick me up from Celine's house.
I slipped on my blue suede trousers and red velvet blazer and made my way into town to meet Celine. She said she had a surprise for me.
I arrived at the clock and noticed she was holding a wedding veil in her hand.

"It's my mum's old veil, I know you didn't have one so I've borrowed it for you. Please look after it though because she'll kill me if she finds out I've taken it," she giggled.

"We're having our hair and makeup done this morning, seeing as nobody else arranged it for you."

"You didn't have to do this, Celine." I said. "Please don't spend your money on this wedding." I felt bad because my heart wasn't in it at all.
"I haven't spent that much," she laughed. "Come and see for yourself."
She grabbed my arm and marched me around to Boots. I took the opportunity to spray her with men's aftershave when she wasn't looking.
She paid a lady at the make-up counter £10, and we both had our make-up done. Celine made me smile, she had a way of taking a scary situation and making it feel safe. I loved her mockery of the traditional wedding morning.

Next, we moved onto the hairdressers, it was a friend of hers and she'd offered Celine a good discount. We got tipsy on two bottles of champagne, and we skipped through Queensgate: me with a face-full of makeup, wedding hair, and a stolen veil on my head. People laughed at us and gave us funny looks but we didn't care.

Jeff, turned up for us half an hour before we had to be at the registry office. I rushed to put the wedding dress on despite trying my best to act as sober as possible. I heard something tear as I wriggled about trying to get it to fit properly. Jeff's wife had been incredibly slim in her much earlier years and the dress only just accommodated me. I didn't worry about the tearing sound, if something had ripped, it wasn't as though she'd ever be wearing it again. She had no children to pass it down to.

We got into Jeff's little car and headed for the registry office. Once it was in sight, I suddenly felt my nerves kick in and I was concerned I'd be sick. I looked at Celine, and she pulled a silly face at me which made me laugh. I think it was her way of reminding me she was there for me.

"Watch the dress when you get out won't you?" Said Jeff. I could barely move. My chest felt tight and it wasn't just because the dress was tight, I was panicking inside.

236

I remember the way my face burned with shame as I walked into the registry office. The ceremony room was tiny and I nearly vomited as I walked in.

Jeff, was holding my arm and I think I may have fallen over had he not been holding me up.

I recognized about ten people in there. Bernie was smiling his stupid smile as usual. I hated him. I was drunk and I wanted to punch him in the face and relish the moment as people laughed.

"Who gives this lady away?" asked the registrar,

"I do," said Jeff, and then he sat down.

The registrar kept looking at me as she read through the service. I wished she'd just stop looking at me. I allowed my mind to drift off, *'I'm bloody stuck with him now aren't I?'* I told myself, *'I'm never going to get away from him now, what would my parents say if they knew I was getting married today?'*

"Moll, are you still with us dear?" asked the registrar.

I nodded and everybody laughed.

"Do you take this man?"

Do I? Do I take this dirty old man to be my *awful* wedded husband? Do I have a fucking choice anymore? I thought. Everybody had let me down and contributed in some way to it getting to this point. I looked over to Celine, she gave me a little reassuring smile. But her eyes told a different story.

"I do." I said quietly, and only because I knew I could get a divorce anytime I wished. It was easier to just go along with it.

The ring was a cheap piece of rubbish from Argos, it was silver with an obnoxious pink cubic Zirconia. I didn't want a wedding band, I wanted to make the whole thing less 'weddingy' as possible. It didn't mean a thing to me. I still thought it would have been cheaper for Bernie to mark me as his territory by pissing up my leg instead of having to pay out for all this crap I had no interest in.

Everybody clapped and it was almost over, I just had to sit on a chair with a smile whilst I signed the register and people took pictures. I didn't smile, I pulled stupid faces instead.

I wished I hadn't found out my place of birth, I wouldn't have gotten my birth certificate and I wouldn't have been married. *'It's only a bit of paper,'* I told myself.

"Wait until you see the hall," said Bernie excitedly. "You won't recognise it."

I hoped I wouldn't, the place was a shit hole at the best of times. You could dress it up however you liked, it would still smell of training classes.

The wedding car that we would use to arrive at the reception was Bernie's Rover 214 with a piece of ribbon thrown across it. It looked like a first prize turd.

The hall smelled sweaty when we arrived. I was made to close my eyes as I was led into the wedding reception, this only heightened my senses making the smell worse.

When I was allowed to open them, I was positively underwhelmed. At the end of the hall was a row of tables where four CRT monitors sat, they were linked to one computer and Bernie's stereo. The music was on low and he was using Windows Media Player's 'visualization effects' to create some kind of disco. The whole thing looked appalling, only I couldn't have cared less. Bernie, thought he'd done a great job.

There was another section of the hall with tables and chairs where a couple of people I recognized from the club were sitting. I barely knew anybody else. The majority of them were Bernie's ex-girlfriends that he'd kept in touch with.

There were crates of warm, shop bought alcohol and bottles of French beer. Pieces of ripped card lay on the floor where the boxes had been opened. It was a complete shambles.

Celine said she'd give me some space so that I could work my way around everybody to thank them for coming. I didn't want her to leave my side, but watched as she sat at the table with the others from the club. I wanted to be a part of the group at that table. To be a guest any somebody's wedding, anybody's but my own.

I didn't know what to do with myself so I decided I'd make a start by taking off my hideous wedding dress. I walked barefooted to the car and took out the bag that contained my clothes. Then I went to the toilets and got changed into some trousers and pink vest top.

"Where's the dress?" asked Jeff, as I entered the hall again.

"Don't worry Jeff, it's been put back safely in its box."

I'd actually left it in a messy pile on the floor of the toilets but he wouldn't find out. I'd sort it later, I decided.

I avoided Bernie like the plague, though he was mainly chatting up his ex-girlfriends anyway so it wasn't difficult. I took a bottle of the terrible French beer and sneaked to the darkened hall next door where I knew they'd stashed a piano away. It was pushed into a corner behind a trampoline but I managed to squeeze through the gap.

I wanted to hide in there until it was all over, until they'd all gone home and I'd have all the next day to ponder my mistake.

I silenced as the door creaked open, bringing the noise from the reception into the room. Jeff peered inside.

"Are you in here, Moll?"

"Go away." I whispered.

"What are you doing in here? After the effort Bernie has made tonight for you, I find you sitting in here. I suggest you get back into the hall and stop being so selfish."

I didn't like Jeff, I hated the way he'd look at me. It churned my stomach and I always thought there was something sinister lurking behind his eyes. Whenever we'd do sparring at the club, even when I was in my early teens, Jeff would hit me incredibly hard in the face, even making my nose bleed once, then he'd smirk about it and not say a single word.

In the smelly hall, people were sat awkwardly at the tables. The music was quiet and all that could be heard was Bernie's drunken ramblings about how intelligent and spiritually enlightened he was. I'd heard enough.

I grabbed a half bottle of whiskey from the side and took it into the community centre reception area. There was a large desk there so I sat against it on the floor, drinking copious amounts of whiskey, insensitive to the way it burned my throat on the way down. If people wouldn't leave, then I'd blot them out one by one with every sip.

I don't remember much after that, besides being violently sick and slightly worrying that Jeff may have found his wifes wedding dress on the toilet floor. I remember a brief moment of sitting in the car outside the caravan and watching Bernie disappear inside. A voice behind me reassured me that I'd be okay. It scared me because I thought I was alone in the car. At the time, I thought perhaps it was an angel. I didn't have the strength to turn around and look. In hindsight, it was probably Celine or one of Bernie's ex girlfriends.

Chapter Twenty Four.

Married life was no different than before. I continued to hand wash clothes on a daily basis. Bernie would continue to assault me behind closed doors, and even occasionally in public if he was sure he was unlikely to see those people again. He began to escort me to Asda every time as he didn't let me leave the house on my own. He'd stand in the aisles and hurl abuse at me, sometimes he'd throw things from off the shelf at me too. It was incredibly humiliating to have all those people staring at me with pity in their eyes. I didn't want their pity - I just wanted them to mind their own business.

Celine saved up the money to buy that return ticket, and not long before Christmas, we said a tearful farewell. I desperately wanted to tell her what was happening with Bernie, but she looked so happy and excited. I couldn't bring myself to stand in the way of her happiness. The day she left, I felt as though I was walking about with a hole in my heart. It was an unbearable pain from the undiscovered depths of my stomach. I knew I'd always be able to contact her as we had each other's email addresses and regularly exchanged emails. I didn't have much to talk to her about though. She was the only good thing in my life, and now she was gone.

With Celine gone, Bernie sensed my vulnerability again.

It was almost Christmas and Bernie decided that the Leicester and Peterborough clubs should come together for a Christmas meal in Leicester. A table was booked for twenty of us at an Indian Restaurant. One of the girls from the club called Rose, had offered to accommodate the ones that were travelling from Peterborough. Bernie had invited George to come along too. He was the only one not drinking as he was underage.

Afterwards, six of us went back to Rose's house and she brought through a couple of bottles of wine. She had to be up early in the morning so she went to bed pretty much as soon as she got in. She was followed closely by Bernie who insisted it was my bed time too.

I told him I would be up soon after, as I wanted to finish my wine downstairs with the others first.

I sat laughing quietly downstairs with George, Charlie, and Rick.

Rick, was only training with us for a short time: he was working towards a sports degree at the university.

I heard the landing creak gently as somebody walked about, then they moved quickly down the stairs. I thought it was Rose. It was her house and I didn't think anyone else would use it in such a manner.

"You'd better get yourself up these fucking stairs right now," said a voice from behind me. It was Bernie's voice. "If you don't come now then I'll drag you up by your hair you fucking bitch."

I could feel my face burning with shame again.
Why was he doing this in front of my friends? I
turned around to answer him and was horrified to
discover that he was stood completely naked in the
doorway.

The others in the room didn't know where to look
and neither did I. I felt so sorry for George who was
only young, but I was fearful for myself too. If he
dared do something like this in front of others, how
much further was he prepared to go behind a closed
door?

I got slowly and shakily to my feet, everybody had
been given a glimpse into the horror that was my
life and I felt so deeply ashamed. I had to go
upstairs to relieve them of this uncomfortable
situation if anything. I felt it was my fault they had
to witness it, it was my problem that I'd let it get to
this stage and now they were all suffering.

Bernie stepped aside to let me pass through the door
before following me out. Then he threw me against
the stairs, grabbed my hair, and manhandled me
upstairs by it.

In the room, he pushed me onto the bed and
grabbed a fistful of my hair, bringing his face close
to mine and sneering.

"You fucking whore, I told you to come to bed
nearly an hour ago. You've been sitting downstairs
flirting with those losers instead. You've made me
look like a right cunt in front of my own fucking
students. If you ever..." he struck me in the stomach
with his fist, "ever do anything like this again," he

brought his face close to mine again, "I *will* fucking kill you."

I'd made such a mess of the crisp white pillowcases Rose had provided, my quiet tears had smudged mascara over them and there was a little blood from hitting my head on the stairs. It was a truly terrible sight. I was sure Rose would understand. I'd heard through another student, tongues loosened at the pub one Friday, that Rose used to be in an abusive relationship. I hurt inside at the thought of it happening in her own house again. What would she have thought of me?

I could hear every whisper and clear of the throat from downstairs. They must have heard everything. They looked up to Bernie, they used to look up to me too, it was unlikely they would now though.

The next morning, I had no idea how I would show my face. Whilst everyone was downstairs silently eating breakfast, I sat upstairs and hoped they would hurry up and leave so I could make a quick escape without the drag of prejudice eyes upon me. Bernie was behaving as though nothing had happened the night before and it sickened me. Rose was silent as I came downstairs; she briefly made eye contact with me then told us all we had to go because she had to pick her daughter up. That was the last time I saw her because she didn't return to training after that night.

I got into the car and we drove back in silence with a young George sitting silently in the back seat.

I'd been married for almost five months and I felt as though my life was coming to an end. If Bernie didn't take it in one of his rages, I may have taken it myself. I often checked the timetables for the next bus with the intention of throwing myself underneath it, but there was a little part of me that wouldn't give up. Bernie cancelled my kickboxing club, he made me ring the parents to explain that he'd revoked my license. There was no way that he could have done this because I was part of an association that had nothing to do with him. He was jealous because I had considerably more students than him after many had left his class. It broke my heart to have to close down the club. The children's parents had all paid money for uniforms, membership and equipment. They were not pleased and I suffered many angry words. Everything I did, it seemed Bernie would always be one step ahead of me, waiting to mess things up for me.

Another Friday came and we were on our way home after the class, we didn't go to the pub that night, people slowly stopped coming as the word spread of what happened at Rose's house. He tried to start teaching children himself but I told him that I didn't agree with it. A row ensued in the car and he pulled over in a layby at the side of the A47. I thought he was going to leave me there as he told me to get out of the car. There was a greasy spoon café in the lay by but it was closed. He grabbed hold of my hair and pulled me behind the greasy café where he attacked me.

I could hear the occasional car pass by quickly, not slowing to look at the car suspiciously abandoned in the lay by with the doors open and the interior light switched on. I could hear the radio playing and the tears ran into the crease of my neck and gathered there. I was glad nobody stopped, they would see what was happening to me and I couldn't bear that humiliation.

We drove back home mostly in silence.

"You bring these things on yourself, Moll," he said, as I cried quietly. "Nobody values your opinion because you behave like a fucking child. You've scared everyone away at the club. Things were fine until you came along, you've messed up my life. I have no contact with my parents now because of you."

I didn't say anything, I wouldn't give that man the pleasure of shooting me down again.

I traded a couple of emails with Celine, she was happy in Brisbane, but was staying in a caravan whilst their house was being built. She'd decided to stay but promised to visit me when she could save up for a return flight. I stopped emailing her after that because I didn't have anything to tell her. I decided that once I sorted my life out and found the strength to make myself safe, I'd be able to chat to her again and explain everything. Until then, I'd not bother her.

Bernie was going over to visit his sleazy friend, James, in Sleaford again. He'd told me to get some coal for he fire whilst he was gone, and he'd left me some money on the side. There was a coal yard in the industrial estate down the road. They charged extra for delivery, but he'd only given me enough to get one big bag that weighed almost as much as me. The fat, greasy men, with their stomach hanging out from underneath their shirts leered at me as I struggled to lift the bag. I dropped it twice before I'd even left the coal yard and they laughed as they watched me struggle. I got past the gates and dropped it again but I carried on. I wanted to cry, this was a stupid idea. They roared with laughter as I picked up the pieces of coal that rolled out into the snow because the bag had split, and I struggled down the road with it. People would beep their horns at me as they drove past. Some were laughing, some stared with pity which I hated more. I dropped it again and the contents spilled out everywhere. It rolled into the road, on the ice and it got wet from the snow. Bernie would be furious that the coal was wet, it was no longer any good until it had dried out.

Then something snapped inside of me. I'd finally had enough.

"Fuck it!" I yelled, at the top of my voice. I kicked the bag until it was nothing but a wet mess in the slush. I didn't care anymore. I'd lost the plot completely - gone stark raving mad. I sobbed my heart out as I ran back towards the mobile home park.

"Are you okay?" a young man on a bike asked me as I ran past him.

"Fuck off and mind your own business." I shouted.

I screamed and kicked the wheelie bin around the garden. I threw the remaining patio set at the shed and it ricocheted off and hit me. This added further to my unstoppable rage. I felt like I had a demon inside of me - that I'd become possessed, any bystander would have agreed. However, my mind and intentions couldn't have been clearer.

I almost kicked the door in as my shaking hands hindered me to unlock the front door. When it did open, I burst into the squalid living room, smashing anything I could find. I ripped the curtains down and I kicked holes in the walls. I was shaking but I was finally feeling something again. I felt alive as I allowed my adrenaline to completely consume me.

The phone rang out on the other end and I knew he'd answer. I waited between the pauses, my fists were clenched and my blood pumped quickly around my body.

"Hello?"

"Dad, it's me, Moll."

I didn't have time for questions or greetings, I could sense the relief in his voice but it mattered not one bit to me.

"I need you to come and pick me up now while he's out of the house. Can you come now? Right now?"

"Yes, of course, what has he done to you? Are you okay?"

"I don't have time for questions, I need you to get off the phone and come now. I don't know what time he'll be back. If he gets here before you do I don't know what'll happen. It turns out he's quite fucking psychotic."

"Okay, I'm coming now. I'll be there within the next two hours, okay?

"Just one more thing, Dad"

"Yes?"

"When you get outside, beep your horn. If you see Bernie's car parked outside then you call the police, okay?"

"What's going on?"

"You just do that okay? He's got all kinds of things in here and he keeps a machete in the boot of his car. Just don't come in here, okay?"

I gave him the directions to the caravan park and hung up the phone.

That was it. I'd endured two and a half years of Bernie's abuse, a simple phone call home could have ended it. I was full of rage and angry at myself too. For once, I felt I had the upper hand.

Fuelled by adrenaline soaked rage, I collected my things in a flurry. I threw my clothes into bin liners and then I took them out again, throwing them across the bedroom. I couldn't take them back with me, they had become tainted by Bernie. I couldn't take anything back with me. I just had to get out of there.

My next stop was Bernie's filing cabinet in the porch. It was a big, metal, ignorant bastard, that I finally managed to break into with some persuasion from a screwdriver.

My VHS was on the top of a pile of many. The label said 'Naughty schoolgirl pays the price.' I went crazy, smashing it on the floor and pulling the tape out from inside. I snapped it as many times as I could until there was an unravelled mess on the floor. I had flashbacks from that evening. The evening I'd lost Stacey as a friend, the night James's silhouette stood in the doorway pleasuring himself whilst Bernie attacked me.

I inspected further, and to my horror, there were more video tapes. They were harmlessly labelled so I assumed the content was likely to be just as horrific. I smashed those up too, and continued pulling the tape out from inside.

There were old love letters from his ex girlfriends, and ladies underwear. He was a complete psychopath. I lost control again and rage had me throwing that cabinet around the porch as though it was a rag doll.

I walked through to the dirty kitchen to write Bernie a note, he didn't deserve an explanation but I felt I had to say something. I found a piece of paper in a drawer and scribbled him a note.

251

"Dear Dirty Old Man,
It has taken me five years to realise that you're
nothing more than a paedophile.
You have tried your best to destroy me but I'm still
young enough to put my life back together.
If you try to find me, I will do what everybody else
failed to do, and call the police. I'll tell the whole
world about you and your friends.
Moll.
Ps. I will never be associated with your disgusting
surname."

I placed the cheap, pink-stoned wedding ring on top
of the note and I left it on the side.
A bang on the door almost made me jump out of my
skin. My adrenaline kicked in again though this
time I would be fighting - not flying.
I looked through the grubby plastic kitchen window.
It wasn't Bernie thank goodness, it was Frank, the
man who owned the mobile home park. He was
another pervert, always trying to get me on my own
in the caravan, making excuses to check the electric
meter every couple of days. His wife was always
covered in bruises. He was a scrawny little man
with a big mouth, (as is so often the case.)
He banged louder on the door and I swung it open
in my continued rage.
    "What the fuck do you want? You pathetic little
piss ant!" I screamed.
He staggered backwards off the steps as though my
words had blown him away.

"I've had a complaint that you've been throwing garden furniture around and smashing things up. If you can't stick to the rules of the park, I'll have to evict you."

"So fucking evict me!" I screamed, "Get the fuck out of this piece of shit garden!"

"I'll call the police you crazy bitch," he shouted back.

"Do it! I'm sure they'd love to hear how you knock your missus about, Frank. Do it! Fill your boots."

"You've got an hour to pack your things and get the fuck off my park before I call them," he shouted, as he walked away.

"Fuck you, Frank," I yelled. I was never going to see him ever again and I didn't care.
I was buzzing. My whole body felt as though it had been given an injection of life. I felt like an eighteen year old, a whole year younger than Bernie had told people I was over two years ago. If only I could erase the last two and a half years of my life, but I couldn't. I had to make changes starting from now. I almost wished Bernie had been there to witness my emancipation.

A green Rover crackled over the gravel as it pulled into the car park. It wasn't Bernie's Rover, it was my dad's. The horn beeped once to let me know he was there.
I didn't even close the door behind me as I left.

My parents didn't get out of the car as I approached. They eyed me as though I was a stranger to them, as though they barely recognized me.

I slumped into the back seat and exhaled a breath of relief.

I wouldn't for a minute allow myself to believe that they had changed their ways. All I knew was that they wouldn't treat me in the manner Bernie had. They were a much safer option.

I hadn't seen them for such a long time and it felt necessary to break the ice.

"How come the badge is missing off the front of your car?" I asked my dad, as though I hadn't been estranged for over two years.

"It's those kids next door to us, I'm convinced they're going to steal it so I take it off at night and bring it in the house. They keep loitering out outside looking at the car. Because I rushed out, I forgot to put it back on."

"Oh," I said, as we pulled away from the mobile home park. I could see nothing had changed much while I'd been away. My dad was still as paranoid as ever.

The familiarity calmed me inside, I was an adult now and nobody could control me anymore.

Epilogue.

The first thing I did when I moved back to Leicester, was get an appointment at the opticians. I was sick to death of not being able to see and I'd always been too scared to ask Bernie for money. Because I hadn't been in full time education and was over sixteen at the time; I wasn't entitled to a free eye test.

I still wouldn't wear glasses, my dad's 'sexetary' comment had scarred me for life.

Instead, I bought some contact lenses and was able to take them away with me the same day.

I vividly remember the moment I put them in and walked out the opticians because I sat on the curb outside and cried.

I heard that Bernie went mad after I escaped, apparently taking horse tranquillizers and verbally abusing anyone who knew him. Another story was that he'd become engaged to a prostitute but these were just rumours.

It was true however, that he left the country and was travelling around Africa and Norway.

Years later my sister, Cara, told me that he'd been hand delivering birthday/anniversary cards to the house; my parents would throw them away so I didn't have to see them.

He has tried to contact me on numerous occasions during these past thirteen years, and once I even replied to him in a civil manner. Oh the grip and fear these people can instil into their victims long after the emancipation.

Since my veil of nativity has lifted, and I have children of my own, the last time he tried to establish contact, my message was quite clear.

I told him that he was a paedophile and was never to contact me again. Perhaps one day I shall get justice and he'll be extradited back to the UK. For now though, I'm happy to be safe.

Moving back home didn't work out, though I'd guessed it wouldn't the day I escaped Bernie. It was merely a stop-gap until I could make a life for myself.

I bought my first house not long afterwards, and later I would be running my own business. My first son came along and changed me beyond description. It was the first time I'd experienced unconditional love, though it opened a few old wounds in relation to my own parents. How is it possible for a parent to not love their child unconditionally? A few years later would see my second arrival and my life would forever be changed.

I still struggle to form bonds with females, perhaps one day this can be resolved. I have a couple of close friends that I know will always be there for me and I don't feel I need much more than that. Life has become about the preservation and protection of the ones I care about and has proved a good role for me.

I rarely have contact with my family now, with the exception of Cara who lives a stone's throw away. I have tried on numerous occasions to build bridges with my family, though they have chosen to ignore my children, despite them being stood only inches away from them at a christening I recently attended. I refuse to allow them to inflict any feelings of rejection upon them, and I'm confident in my ability to keep my children safe and nurtured.

Whilst I cannot change the things that happened in my past, I can certainly use my experience to prevent it from happening to many more vulnerable children.
Despite leaving school with no qualifications whatsoever, I managed to obtain a diploma in social work, and have worked successfully with children who have been victims of abuse.

I heard Beryl got a nose job, though she told everybody she'd had an accident that made her eyes bruise and nose requiring strapping up. I've seen photographs and believe she looks better for it. Not because I believe cosmetic surgery was her answer; but because for once in her life she smiles genuinely in her pictures.

Beth, met a man that behaved very much like my father, who would stay in bed every day. She had two beautiful children, and after introducing her to a friend of mine, she is now happily married and they have a lovely home together. Unfortunately, her new best friend is married to an ex of mine, so I didn't get an invite to her hen party. I did get a wedding invite but declined because my children weren't invited.

A similar situation happened with Beryl too, I didn't get a hen night invitation, though saw the photo's on Facebook with my family laughing and joking together.

I'm certain they all have their own stories that have shaped them into the people they are today. I love my life now and I truly wish them all the best of luck and happiness.

Bernie's friend 'Brian,' sadly passed away in 2007, though before then he had become my friend and new instructor since escaping Bernie, (yes I did actually turn up to his classes!) He despised Bernie when the revelations came to light after I left; it was Brian who urged me to speak to my GP about counselling.

I attended Brian's funeral in Southampton. After years of being called a hypochondriac, he suffered a massive heart attack in his sleep and didn't wake up. He left behind a lovely partner and beautiful baby girl who I hope one day will learn what a thoroughly decent man he was. Me and Bernie would sometimes call at his shared house before training on Friday's and he'd make us dinner. It was always beans on toast, with a sprig of parsley. That memory will forever be in my heart and I wrote in down in his book of tribute.

My dad was diagnosed with cancer of the oesophagus in 2003, though he pulled through and made a full recovery. During this time we were on speaking terms. After his recovery, he went back to his old tricks and we spoke not a single word. Then he crashed his car and broke his back. The fire crew said that it was a miracle he survived, and if there had been any travelling passengers they would have been killed outright.
He pulled through again and we no longer speak again. I found myself going around in circles with him and he never made any attempt to see his grandchildren. He did end up on his own.

My mum remarried a lovely man who I have a lot of respect for. I broke down at her wedding and she promised things would be different, that she would email me and I could take my family to her house for dinner like the others did. Unfortunately, that email must have gotten itself lost in cyberspace.

I'm no longer as naïve as I used to be, and I no longer desire acceptance from the people who will never accept me. I may still be the shameful, family secret in their eyes, but I have now told my story and my voice has been heard.

Bernie gets no further mention in my book, he has ceased to exist to me now.

I eventually tracked Celine down after losing her email address. Here are a couple of genuine emails we exchanged. *Email addresses have been censored.

*****

Sent: Wednesday, February 21, 2007 10:46 PM
Subject: hey mr dj...

hi Celine!!

hey mr dj put a record on....
omg please don't ask me how i found your email address because it's taken me ages!!! lol
i hope you remember me, you were after all, a bridesmaid at my wedding in peterborough.
i hope you're ok, im contactable on this email address which i check everyday, i also have myspace if you have a profile on there
http://www.myspace.com/-------------
i hope to hear back from you soon, it's been too long my lovely

Moll
:) xxx

*****

Sent: 02 March 2007 03:52:41
To: -------------------------
Moll! Molly! So good to hear from our mr dj......
what kinda mischief
have you been getting up to? ;-) hehe
I've been thinking about you...couldn't do much
about it though cus hotmail
trashed my account -I hadn't checked the mail
regularly enough and they
deleted my contacts the B*** (bad people!)

Email is a bit tricky as we're in a caravan in the
countryside (Caboolture,
Queensland, Australia) using solar energy so no
telephone line! So will take
a while to reply to emails. Still working on my uni
thesis - one year to
go!
So what have you been up to? Are you running the
pub? You're looking sexy -
as usual!
Tell me your news. And I'll write more soon
Lots of love
Celine :-)

*****

From: -------------------
Sent: 02 May 2008 09:01:28
To: -------------------
Hey Mr DJ Moll
So sorry it's taken so long to write to you. Been living in a caravan and trying to get the power, telephone, internet etc sorted as well as complete this crazy thesis plus heaps more stressy things I won't bore u with. But still a whole year since I wrote to u last! I'll kung fu myself for a few minutes as penance! Do you still practise the kicks and punches by the way?

How is the studying going? Did you get a place closer to Leicester? How is little ----------? We've got a wireless modem in the caravan now so will be able to phone you after the 10th May when we have some download gigs...any time better for u? There's a 10 hour difference here. so in the uk 9am is 7pm in Oz...its a bit crazy!.
And I'm on skype now - could type to you too . our user name is
 ----
and hotmail is ---------------------
Lets catch up soon

Love
Celine :-)

*****

From: ----------------------------

Sent: 02 July 2012 17:38:57

To: ----------------------------

Outlook

2 attachments (total 1518.6 KB)

Hey Celine,

Been such a long time again and loads has happened.

I was looking through my old emails because I wanted to get in touch.

How the devil have you been? Hows uni stuff going?

I have 2 little lads now, ------ (8) ------- (3) both little tyrants :) (I've attached mugshots)

it's been sooooo long!

Do you think you'll ever come back to visit the UK? I'd love to come over to Oz at some point but am probably a couple of years away from that with ----- ------ being so young.

Bet you don't remember dancing round your living

room to Delirium - Silence? Every time I hear it, it reminds me of that moment haha.

Look forward to hearing from you soon, hope you're well :)

Loadsa love

Moll xxxx

*****

From: --------------------------------
Sent: 28 August 2013 19:22:30
To: --------------------------------
I miss you so much. Love Moll :(xxxxx

The e-mail dated 2nd May 2008 would be the last I'd hear from Celine. In 2010 she sadly took her own life and I wouldn't discover this until 2012, a whole two years later, whilst trying to track her down again because my emails to her were being returned.
The pain of discovering the death of a loved one through an online obituary is one that takes a long time to heal. I'd been so wrapped up, enjoying my own life that I assumed she'd always be there at the end of an email at my convenience.
I desperately wish I'd added her on Skype to have seen her face just one last time. My hotmail account

containing many more of our email exchanges prior to these, became deactivated as I hadn't logged in.

Celine had sent me a photograph of her wedding day. It was of her wearing the dress we bought on our shopping trip to Monsoon on the evening of the fashion show, the pink mandarin style dress that she loved so much. I lost the photograph along with the emails but the image will stay in my heart forever. She was there when I needed her the most; I wish as an adult that I would have been able to help her through her problems as she did for me. I never knew they existed; she always hid it behind a smile.

I refused to speculate the circumstances surrounding her suicide; I don't believe anybody could possibly imagine the torment one must feel to take their own life. I'd speculated enough about Darren's suicide and I realised that whilst I did, there was no chance of my grieving properly. I just didn't want to let go of either of them. Now I know that I don't have to because I'll always keep the best of them in my memories.
Nobody can tell us when it's okay to stop grieving a loved one, it is however, fair to allow ourselves to adjust to life without them. After all, they would have only wished for our happiness.

We often holiday on the east coast, which means briefly passing through Peterborough. It used to fill me with dread as I'd associated the place with abuse. They were feelings I'd put in my own mind

though and I slowly came to realise that I was
wrong.
However haunting the place looks when the fog
rolls in, and despite feeling like I'm stuck in a time
warp whenever we drive past; it's a city standing in
its own right.

There has been so much tragedy in my life, there
have been so many wonderful things happen too. To
say my life is perfectly balanced now would be
premature of me, as we never know what's lurking
around the corner.
What I do know, is that right now I'm happy, and
apparently I make others happy too which is
important to me.

It's dismal and drizzling outside as I type, but I'm
no longer looking out of a plastic kitchen window
as a scared child. I'm watching the world go by and
I'm finally glad to have found my place in it.

My Poem for Darren (Moll, aged 12)

If I had a wish to use today,
I'd turn back time to yesterday.
My friend was hurting but he didn't say,
So I couldn't help him in any way.

Even the adults are crying now,
They couldn't help either
They didn't know how.
He didn't say how he was feeling low,
I could have helped him, though I'll never know.

Now up to heaven my friend will fly
He'll light up the clouds
And he'll dance in the sky.
And when it's my turn
And I depart,
I know he'll be waiting
To mend my heart.

Made in the USA
Middletown, DE
16 April 2018